AF316829

The Beautiful Addiction

Dr. Zeev Gilkis

Producer & International Distributor
eBookPro Publishing
www.ebook-pro.com

The Beautiful Addiction
Zeev Gilkis

Illustrations by Omri Gilkis

Contact: zeev.gilkis@yahoo.com
ISBN 9789655752410

The
Beautiful
Addiction

Passing Through the Marathon Wall for the 70th Birthday

DR. ZEEV GILKIS

CONTENTS

March 1st, 2020. It is my 69th birthday!
And yes! I must admit, I'm addicted! But it is a beautiful
addiction, as you will come to understand soon.

PROLOGUE

In my first two books, *Unlock Bliss: A Memoir of Getting Happier* and
The Secret Of Life: A Memoir of Getting Younger, I shared with the
readers the story of my struggle with cancer, some important and
original thoughts and understandings about life and happiness, like
"age doesn't matter!" and many more.

In very unpretentious language, I described some key processes in
the brain, the role of the immune system and how to take care of it,
the story about my beginning in sporting activities in my sixties, and
more good stuff.

In my third book, *Running Back In Time, Discovering the Formula to
Beat the Aging Process and Get Younger*, I told my readers how starting
as coach potato, I came to run a half marathon, and then another one,
then a third one, and then my fourth half marathon.

In that book, I also shared with the readers the idea about an unusual
present for my 70th birthday – running my first full marathon!

Let me give you some background. This might not be so unusual if I
was a "natural born" athlete. But I was quite the opposite for most of

my life; a mathematician by education, the only "sports" I participated in were chess and bridge tournaments.

I'm also a cancer survivor; I had Stage 3 colorectal cancer (out of four), with a 30% probability rate of survival. I received chemotherapy, radiotherapy and underwent two surgeries. Since then, yearly tests show that I'm okay and the cancer hasn't recurred.

Some five years ago, I had a major turning point in my life, and I became interested in sports. The key motivation was to strengthen my immune system by engaging in a-little-to-moderate physical activity; 10 to 20 minutes a day.

This was a good plan. Many studies confirm that even moderate physical activity three to four times a week dramatically improves the robustness of our immune system, keeps us healthy and in good shape. This is highly recommended for everyone.

Soon after I began, however, the intensity of my activities grew very quickly. I was really enjoying myself, I felt good and was motivated to do more.

The first major milestone was on May 6, 2017 when I competed in a triathlon for the first time - at the age of 66. It was a Sprint Triathlon, i.e., only half of the Olympic distances: swimming 750 meters, biking 20 km and running 5 km.

Soon thereafter, a major injury in my right knee was diagnosed, a double tear in the medial meniscus. I had to undergo surgery and was forced to stop my sport activities. I lost half of the meniscus in the surgery and was told not to run anymore.

But I couldn't help myself; I couldn't give up running. After a few months I returned to running, swimming and biking, and competed in a triathlon, this time with full Olympic distances (swimming 1.5 km, biking 40 km and running 10 km).

Unfortunately, a year later, in summer of 2018, I had my second major injury. A partial tear in the patellar tendon, in the same right knee. Again, I was told by the surgeon as well as "a second opinion" orthopedist, to give up running.

I obeyed this recommendation for two full months. But then I began again, increasing the intensity of the activities very slowly and gradually, from square one; running initially one kilometer, after a week two kilometers, and so on.

Following my 68th birthday decision, I began training seriously. The turning point was on November 1, 2019, when I ran my first half marathon. In the following months, I ran three more half marathons. The fourth one was in February of 2020, with a finishing time of two hours and eleven minutes.

So, here I am, proving that despite having had no physical sport background in the first six decades of my life and despite fighting cancer and going through two major injuries, I made it halfway toward achieving my goal – to run the first full marathon on my 70th birthday. Mind over matter!

I like the following citation attributed to Walt Disney, "If you can dream it, you can do it!" My dream was to run a full Marathon! And isn't my 70th birthday the ideal occasion?! ☺

Now I'm beginning the hard work toward this ambitious goal and I'm starting this diary to share with you, the reader, the long and winding road ahead.

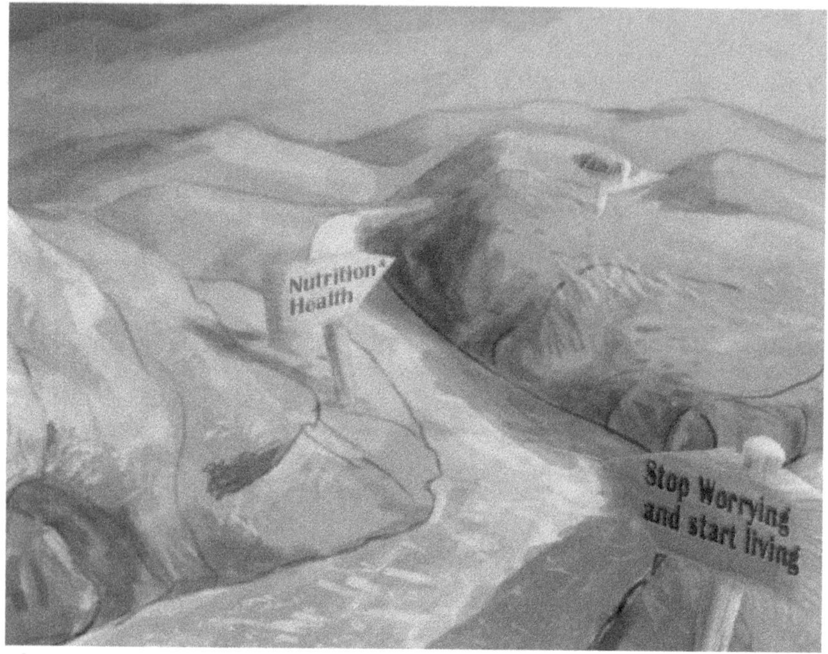

I believe it will be interesting and that we both will learn more about running and about life. I'm sure that those who run will definitely enjoy reading this book. Those who are considering running will get huge encouragement and lots of practical tips from this book, how to enjoy running while avoiding injuries. Those who never thought to run, but are curious and open-minded, should enjoy this book, too.

CHAPTER 1

The Addiction

March 1ˢᵗ, 2020
My 69ᵗʰ birthday! Yes! I admit it I'm addicted! But this is a beautiful addiction, as you will see soon.

One year has passed since my decision and during the 69ᵗʰ year of my life, I've made major progress on the path to accomplish my goal. But the half marathon is only half of the story.

Now I begin the second half of my journey toward the full marathon, one year from now.

The second half is not equal to the first half - and running each additional kilometer, beyond the half-marathon's 21 km, will be a challenge. Eventually, around the 32nd kilometer, I will meet "The Wall!" Many marathon runners "hit the wall" and can't continue.

How I will perform at this challenging meeting?! (What is the wall, you ask? Keep reading and you'll find out!)

Along with the plans and dreams, I'm starting this diary, sharing with

YOU – The Reader - all the ups and downs I expect to encounter on this long and challenging journey. Be my companion in this adventure and you will see that you, too, can achieve anything you truly want.

So, what am I addicted to?! I'm addicted to running, to the endorphins released when I make a major prolonged effort, to the joy and elation that comes along with the process, and feeling that my body is in harmony with my mind, obeying my crazy dreams and wishes. I'm in real unity with my body! I mean, my mind is!

Rene Descartes (1596–1650) was the most important figure in the field of philosophy of mind. Although he was also a great mathematician and scientist, he is best known for his proof of existence, "I think therefore I am." (**Cogito ergo sum,** in Latin.) A key notion of his philosophy is the **dualism of body and mind**.

During my long physical activities, I feel a true union of my body and mind. So, for me, they are not separate entities. I love the excitement before running and the satisfaction after.

This feeling of joy is with me after the activity, during the day, and in the evening when I sit to summarize the day. These feelings and my perfect health since I began training seriously, make me happy.

There is a certain beauty in not knowing; when I began to implement my plan, nobody, not even I, myself, could know how it would end.

I will definitely enjoy this journey, and I'm sure that you as my companion, will enjoy too!

CHAPTER 2

Corona And Me

March 2020

For the last few years, I've gone on ski vacations at the beginning of March. I go to Szklarska Poręba, a small ski town in the Karkonosze Mountains in the Sudetes in southwestern Poland, along the border with the Czech Republic.

I've picked the beginning of March for three reasons:

1. It is the end of the season so there are less people, shorter lines and the slopes are not as crowded.
2. At this time there is usually still snow up in the mountains, so there are reasonable skiing conditions.
3. It's not too cold; the coldest it usually gets is -5° Celsius, or 25° Fahrenheit.

This year, the winter was very light and for most of the season there hasn't been enough snow for skiing. But I got lucky, and there were snow showers the week before I left for vacation, so I came at a perfect time.

I really love snow and skiing, the white background, experiencing a true winter, the motion on the skis and the speed. For me, skiing is like dancing on the snow. And if it snows while I'm skiing, it is really beautiful!

Maybe I love it because it also reminds me of my childhood. Although I wasn't a skier when I was a young boy in Poland, I did grow up with white winters every year.

As with the other sports activities I described above, I began skiing a bit late, when I was 63. Each year there is further progress and more joy and satisfaction.

March 9, 2020

On my lovely ski vacation. But all at once, the world seems to be entering a monumental crisis. We've just learned of a pandemic called COVID-19. From total globalization only a short while ago, suddenly countries are imposing limitations on flights and travel.

It started with flights from China being cancelled, but now travel is also being restricted from other countries, where more cases of coronavirus are being reported. I suddenly realized that I'm losing control and my ability to fly may very soon be limited. From that moment on, my subconscious took control, and within a few minutes, I decided to cut my vacation short.

It is 8 pm in the evening and there isn't much I can do. I tried to change my flight on LOT's website, the Polish Airlines I had flown on, but it didn't work. Some good came out of entering the website, however – it's possible to call the airline from 5 am and on!

March 10, 2020

I was on the phone this morning at 5 am. After a long wait of almost an hour, I succeeded in talking to a customer service representative and got a ticket home for Thursday, March 12th. I currently have 48 hours until the flight. I need to organize things, check out and drive some 500 km (or just over 300 miles) from Szklarska Poręba to Warsaw.

After changing my flight, I also manage to change my hotel booking and notify the car rental company of my date changes.

March 11, 2020

Wednesday, 6 am, I'm in the car. I thought I'd be able to enjoy slightly lighter traffic by leaving so early, at least at the beginning of the trip. The drive to Warsaw, including three stops, takes me seven hours and goes smoothly.

I'm spending tonight in Warsaw.

March 12, 2020

Thursday morning. I just got to the airport and I see on the board that many flights are being canceled. My heart begins beating quickly. After a few seconds, I see my flight – it's still on schedule and I'm okay!

Home!

It appears that I have succeeded in catching one of the last flights from Poland to Israel. The small plane was almost empty, less than 20 people.

The authorities have also requested to close the hotels… I was really lucky to have left at what truly appears to have been the last minute. Intuition and fast decisions…

Now that I've arrived in Israel, I have to quarantine for two weeks at home, in isolation. I can see the positive; I'm been granted an opportunity to catch up on many plans I had on my never-ending "to do list."

One of them was to write this book.☺

I'm building a daily routine which will include two sessions of exercising for at least one hour each, 2-3 meditation sessions between 30 to 40 minutes each, playing chess and bridge against my computer, reading and writing.

The world is undergoing a metamorphosis, from almost complete globalization to near total isolation. Isolation on the country level and isolation on the individual level. It feels as though the world will never be the same.

For example, it is very hard to imagine a return to the peak of tourism, after all the fears we are exposed these days.

There may also be a major shift from the extreme spending on almost everything to a mode of survival, amidst rising unemployment and an awareness that more unknown threats, like another virus, can show up...

Despite the situation, I still have strong motivation to exercise. First, because I believe this is the best remedy for any illness, and for fighting viruses in particular.

This is mainly due to the crucial contribution of physical activity to the strength of the immune system. I wrote about the relation between exercising and the robustness of the immune system in my other book, *The Secret of Life*.

Second, I've set the goal of running my first marathon for eleven months from now. If I don't exercise, it will not happen.

Third, I do have more time now. ☺

March 17th

I was running in any conditions; cold, hot, rain, no rain.
One day earlier this week, I planned a 10 km run, but right after I began, a heavy rain came down and gave me a cold bath. A thought crossed my mind: maybe I should just cut my run to 5 kilometers?

But my subconscious immediately rejected this idea. I recalled a night in the army many years ago, when we were navigating in a heavy rain during the officers' course. A rumor had spread that we could just stop and go back to the base. When we did, our commander was furious and sent us back to the cold darkness and the rain to conclude the mission.

That was a great lesson: A mission must be accomplished. I'll never forget that night and the lesson.

Exercising at home includes cycling on my bike on a trainer simulating real biking, various drills with weights and many exercises on the floor. (See green trainer in picture below.)

And a lot of planks. Planks don't require any equipment:

The Plank Exercise: *Lie face down with legs extended and elbows bent and directly under shoulders; clench your hands. Feet should be hip-width apart, and elbows should be shoulder-width apart. Contract your abs (abdominal muscles), then tuck your toes to lift your body (forearms remain on the ground); you should be in a straight line from head to heels. Hold or as long as you can.*

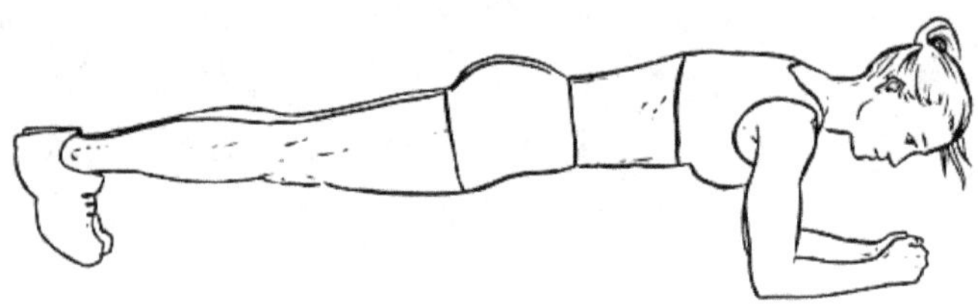

We begin with 30 seconds, next time 40, then 50 and after a few weeks you can hold three minutes.

I've achieved a record time of six minutes!

From time to time, I sneak out for a run on the beach. I do it in the early morning, around 5:30 am. There are very few people out during such early morning hours, and I keep a substantial distance from them. When I get back to my apartment, I don't use the elevator but rather climb the stairs up 12 floors. This way I don't bump into anybody. Interestingly, climbing staircase causes a very fast rise in the heart rate.

Friday, March 27th
Free from isolation!

But it is only psychological, as severe restrictions are imposed on the whole population. We are permitted to go out for a few minutes, however not farther than one hundred meters from home. But 100 meters in each direction makes for a 200-meter "running track."

Also, the time is limited, so I did it 10 times: 2 km in 9 minutes.☺

I'm beginning to understand that this is the new reality:
100 meters around the block. That's it.

And, of course, not seeing people. Nobody. Not even closest family, as each of us lives in a different town. We do communicate digitally and by phone, but we are not able to meet anybody in person.

I'm putting together a new routine:
First, running more - every other day.
Waking up before 5 am and being out by 5:15.

I find that the streets are empty at that hour, so I can extend my "100 meter" limits. I'm now running 5 km up to 10 km, cumulatively at least 25 km per week.

Later on during the day, I do another two or three sessions on the trainer, or just do floor exercises with or without weights.

My goal is to hit at least two hours of exercise daily. And I'm managing to meet this goal.

I also built a setup for my surfboard and use it to simulate swimming, as I can't currently go to a pool or the beach.

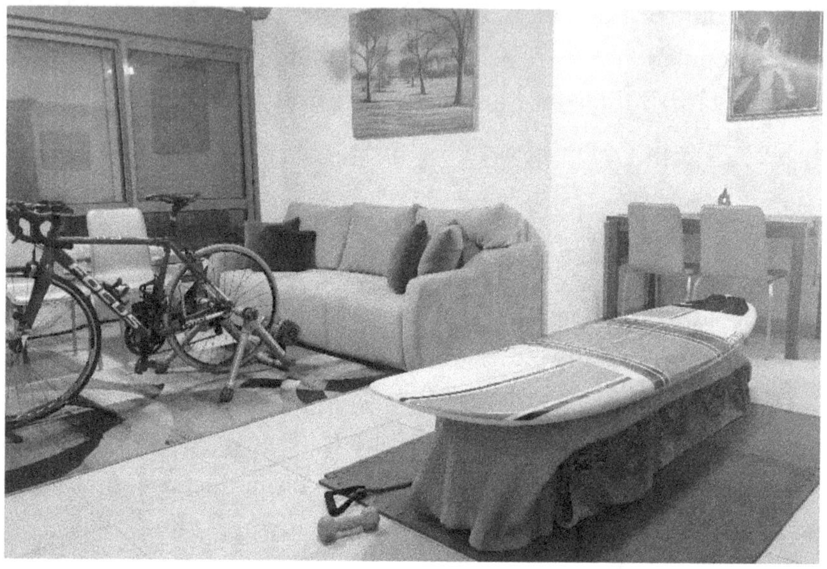

I'm dividing the physical activity into three or four sessions during the day. This is as a result of me being bored after a half-hour or so. But it has the advantage of keeping me active throughout the day.

Regarding muscles, I believe they don't care whether I exercise continuously for 60 minutes, or in two sessions of 30 minutes each.

Regarding the cardio-vascular system, it is making a difference in that I'm not getting tired enough in a half-hour and my heart rate doesn't rise much. But my cardiovascular system is in a pretty good shape from the running, so all-in-all, the combination seems to be quite effective.

Running in the dark has the advantages of being alone and enabling longer distances, but it has its disadvantages too. One day last week I met a pack of wild boars, crossing the street some 20 meters (or about 65 feet) away from me. It was quite frightening!

Luckily for me, a turned-over garbage can drew their attention more than a skinny old man. I ran really fast and managed to escape.

But I can't forget that incident, and every morning while running in the darkness, I keep a look out for the wild pigs, all the while thinking where I should climb in case I meet them again.
This morning, an early-rising policeman stopped me. But I was able to explain myself, and he let me go.

April 12th
I came back from Poland a month ago. During this month, I haven't met one person. The last time I saw my family was before flying to my ski vacation in Poland, on my 69th birthday, six weeks ago.

I once had a dream to become a monk in Tibet. Just to live and meditate a lot during the day. In full quiet.

So, maybe this dream came true?!

I'm alone. It's quiet.

I do meditate a lot. At least twice a day. Instead of my former half-hour routine, I do at least one hour each session. I don't complain.

I'm a kind of a lonely wolf. (BTW, my name – Zeev – means a wolf in Hebrew. ☺) I like to be alone, although in normal times, I also enjoy some company. Especially that of family and friends.

In addition to the sport activities, mediation and preparing my healthy food, I'm also back to my main hobby and area of interest – neuroscience.

I watch lectures, read papers and I went back to my many notes with various ideas. The rest of the time, I play bridge and chess against my computer.

All in all, I feel well, my physical condition is better than ever and I am managing to deal well with the loneliness.
One of the tricks is my daily routine.

The other is setting short-term goals. So, every day I know what I shall accomplish by the end of the day. Both tricks are warmly recommended for our daily life in general.

CHAPTER 3

The Temple Of The Soul

My dear friend Tal wrote to me once, "As the years pass, I do appreciate more and more, the importance of maintaining the body in good shape."

The phrase "*Mens sana in corpore sano,*" or "a healthy mind in a healthy body," was originally coined by the Roman poet Juvenal during the first century CE. So, already two thousand years ago, smart people came to this wise conclusion!

My dear friend Avigdor commented on my book *Running Back in Time* that I put too much emphasis on physical activity and not enough value on intellectual activity and challenges.

Dear Avigdor: I do not disagree – intellectual activity is very important and valuable too. But still, **the body is "The Temple of The Soul!"**

Without a well-functioning body, one's intellectual activity cannot function at its best. I claim that neuro-degenerative brain disorders can be prevented by physical activity.

It is already scientifically proven that physical activity is correlated with neurogenesis (the birth of new neurons) in the hippocampus. And the hippocampus is critically involved in memory processing. Thus, sports activity supports memory.

Another key value of sports and activity is supporting good blood circulation; we need the smallest blood vessels to reach to the most distant and crowded areas in the brain. The billions of neurons and glia cells are packed in the brain extremely densely. It is not easy for the tiny blood vessels to make their way in this "crowd" and get through to all the most distant areas of the brain.

To make it even more challenging, the brain is at the top of our body, so there is a need of extra power to push the blood up (as opposed to legs, for example). That's why it is a good habit to stand on the head, from time to time; I do it every morning, but only for a minute or two. Areas that do not receive the best blood flow, which supplies oxygen and nutrients, may begin degenerating.

Therefore, while not ignoring intellectual activity, I'm back to my mission: attempting to convince everybody who is open and ready to listen, regarding the crucial importance of sporting activities.

And of course, first to convince you – the reader. Hopefully, my story will serve as a supporting argument☺.

CHAPTER 4

The First Step Toward The Marathon

April 30th

The time to cross the Rubicon has come. If I want to run the full marathon in ten months from now, I have to begin making some progress. The first step, cross the half marathon barrier — 22 km — today.

I know I can do it. After all, I ran a half marathon four times in the last six months. So, adding another 800 – 900 meters shouldn't be a deal breaker. The questions are: How difficult will it be? What will hurt and how much? How will it feel?

I wake up early, 4:30 am. I like this quiet morning time.

The first 15 km are okay, although quite slow. I'm very careful, I take small steps, keep a low cadence. In the last seven km, the "mechanics" make some trouble. The "pump" is fine, average heart rate is below 150. Easy breathing. I have the energy, no problem. The usual suspects behave, both the right knee and the left forefoot – no pain!

But the left knee, maybe envying its right brother, is quite painful. I have to really slow down, even walking for a minute or so. Eventually I finish in two hours and forty-eight minutes. Really slow.

The recovery is very fast, as always. Beginning to think about the next step: 24 km on May 27th.

I put the "mask" after my run. ☺

CHAPTER 5

The 5 Am Club And Setting Goals

Robin Sharma is a globally respected humanitarian. Widely considered one of the world's top leadership and personal optimization advisors, his clients include famed billionaires, professional sports superstars and many Fortune 100 companies. The author's #1 bestsellers such as *The Monk Who Sold His Ferrari*, *The Greatness Guide* and *The Leader Who Had No Title*, have been translated into over 92 languages, making him one of the most broadly-read writers alive today.

In his book *The 5 AM CLUB: Own Your Morning. Elevate Your Life*, he very convincingly presents the advantages of rising early. I definitely belong to this club and warmly invite you to join us. ☺

Assuming 6 am is a quite common wake-up time, rising at 5 am gives you another private hour, dedicated only to you. In this additional hour, you are with yourself; you can perform some sport activities, meditate or just be by yourself in the quietness of the early morning. Maybe review the goals for the day and for the near future?

Setting clear goals enables us to push ourselves to perform at our best. To be practical, it is good to set goals for the day, the week, the month, the year and beyond. Goals should be written down and clearly defined. They should not be set too low, so that the achievement of the objective will have merit, but at the same time, not too high, so that it will be achievable. Advancement toward goals, even if progress is slow, is a great source of positive feelings and happiness.

Defining goals is an important technique. In a once popular strategic management model, Management by Objectives, a mnemonic acronym – SMART - was broadly used as a guide for setting objectives.

S.M.A.R.T. stands for:
Specific
Measurable
Ambitious
Realistic
Time-bound

The first-known use of the term occurred in the November 1981 issue of Management Review by George T. Doran. The principal advantage of S.M.A.R.T. objectives is that it is easier to understand them and to know when they have been achieved.

Coordinating expectations is relevant to everybody and for almost everything, but the most important thing is coordinating expectations with ourselves. Failing to meet our own expectations causes frustration and impairs motivation.

When I run on a familiar track, I run faster. This is because I can plan better and pace myself accordingly. My expectations are well coordinated. But when I try out a new track, I'm more careful and I run more slowly, in order to preserve energy for the unexpected. In this case, the expectations aren't coordinated and my performance is compromised.

The most important coordination of expectations is with ourselves - what do we expect from ourselves.

Achieving our goals is crucial for our feeling of satisfaction and happiness. Maybe our level of happiness can be perceived by how much we achieve or even exceed the goals we set. On the flip side, if we miss a goal, the level of the disappointment, unhappiness or even frustration, may be proportional to the gap between the target and the outcome.

In a "mathematical" formula, the level of happiness could be defined as:

H=A/E

H standing for happiness (or satisfaction)
A – standing for achievement
E – standing for the expectations (the goal we set)

I.e., the more the achievement exceeds the expectations, the happier we are.
I joined the "5 AM Club" when I started competing in triathlons. In order to be at the start line at 6:30 am, I have to be at the event site no later than 6 a.m., and before that, I must organize things at home, take care of my physiological needs, and drive to the event's place. So, many times it meant rising even at 4 am, or earlier. But it's so early only on these special occasions.

May 14th
My daily routine now begins with rising around 5 am. BTW, I'm not using alarm clocks on a daily basis, only for events. To wake up at 5 am, I'm going to bed around 11 pm, allowing my body six hours of

sleep. I found this amount of sleep time optimal for me, by experimenting on myself. For two weeks, I let myself wake up without using an alarm clock. I wrote down my natural wake up time and how many hours I slept. It came out to six hours with very small deviations.

It appears that the vast majority of the population sleeps between 6 and 7 hours. Therefore, my routine now is: I say good night at 11 pm - with rare exceptions because of social events in the evening - and good morning at 5 am.

I love this early morning hour of between 5:00 and 6:00. The quietness. No disturbance, no phone calls or WhatsApps. ... I use it mainly for sport activities, followed by a shower and meditation.

But sometimes it is useful for other purposes too. When I had to leave Poland because of the suddenly imposed corona flight restrictions, I could call LOT Airlines at 5 am, before others, and get my ticket. I also could leave the hotel, for the long drive at 6 am, after all my preparations, and enjoy just some light traffic.

During the strictest corona days, despite the fact that it wasn't allowed, I would run at 5:30 am, as there were no people (and no police...) on the streets. Then, I would do my basic food shopping before 7 am. Usually, someone would let me in before the actual 7 am opening hour, so I would have the whole store for myself. But these were exceptional days.

In more normal times, I start my day mainly by indulging with my green tea in the quietness of the 5 am hour, some sport and meditation. As a valuable byproduct, it regulates perfectly my sleeping habits; going to bed at 11 pm is perfect for my body and I fall asleep in seconds.

All in all, warmly recommended.

CHAPTER 6

The Second Step, 24 Km

May 27th, 2020
According to THE PLAN, today I'll run 24 km for the first time. Two kilometers longer than the 22 km I ran four weeks ago.

I wake up at 4 am, this time using the alarm clock.
Although I am usually an early riser, 4 am is a bit exceptional… I wake up so early in order to begin the journey as early as possible, hopefully running most of the distance before the heat becomes unbearable.

At a quarter past five, I'm on my track – the Haifa beach promenade. Some warming up and stretching, and I go.

I begin very easy. Let the body to continue the warm-up and my brain to understand what I want from it.
My mind knows…

I make this subtle distinction between the mind, which is a kind of my soul, and the brain, which is a more "technical organ," best compared to a computer. In my neuroscience research, I do claim that the mind resides in the brain, but this is another topic. Maybe for the next book.☺

The first 10 km are okay. I've run this distance many times. But the brain knows by now, that this time the 10 km are only a fraction of today's journey. This could explain why I'm running so slowly. It is as though the brain is planning a wise and "economical" use of my energy.

It takes me over an hour to finish the 10 km. Slow. Twelve kilometers, half of the distance planned for today, takes me 75 minutes. Slow, but still alright.

My goal is to run the 24 km in three hours. So far, I'm "on time." I like my path, and the quiet of the early morning.

Some people begin to show up. But not many. When I run early in the morning, many times beginning in the darkness, and I see others walking or running, it makes me feel good. Some of the faces become familiar with time, despite the fact that we never talk. Sometimes we might smile, or say hello.

It's like a virtual community of early risers, sharing the passion of being out and in motion. I like belonging to this beautiful community.

After 17 km, my right knee begins to complain. This is the knee which was injured twice. In the operation, I lost half of the meniscus (and was told to stop running). What I find strange is that the surgery was on the medial (inner) part and the pain is on the outer side.

Maybe there is a kind of a balance issue? I decrease the length of my stride and run more slowly. I am trying to be very accurate with each stride, as much as possible.
By accurate, I mean not splaying the foot, not pushing off the toes, and "throwing" the foot back. The idea is to minimize the contact between the foot and the ground, just touching the ground gently and immediately lifting the ankle.

All of these efforts enable me to finish the 24 km. It took me three hours and eight minutes, a pace of 7:50. All in all, I liked the experience. If not for the pain in my knee, I could run more.

At this pace, I figure, I would finish a full marathon in 5 hours and 30 minutes. Still okay, as the official marathon cut-off is six hours (i.e., a pace of up to 8:30 min/km).

But my goal is to finish in five hours or less. This means a pace of 7:07 min/km. Seems that I'll have to adjust my goal.

If I was running 24 km at 7:50, my time would most probably be even slower in the full marathon. So, let's compromise; I set the maximal pace to 8 minutes per kilometer, meaning I could finish in 5 hours and 40 minutes.

Although this time will be 40 minutes longer than my original, wishful thinking, I'll achieve my main goal - to run the full 42.2 km marathon distance!

The key obstacle in my way is the pain in my knee, and the question is whether, by running such long distances, I am taking an unreasonable risk, as the two orthopedists I consulted with have told me.

My thoughts switch between optimism and pessimism. When the pain begins, I become worried whether I am going to be able to continue running long distances.
When I finished the 24 km, I was more optimistic. The recovery was fast; 48 hours after the run, I was on my bike.

May 30^{th,} 2020
Seventy-two hours after my 24 km run, I am running again – 7 km. But the knee hasn't felt right from the beginning of this short run. Maybe it was too early and I should have waited another day?

But after two kilometers, the pain has gone ("gone with the wind"…) and I am happy.

The plan will continue unchanged; I extend the distance by two kilometers every four weeks, while between these 20+ km runs, I add a 15+ km run, and of course several 7-10 km runs.

The next steps:
June 10th – 17 km
June 24th – 26 km
June 28th – June 30th – a surprise ☺
July 8th – 18 km
July 22nd – 28 km
And then we'll see…

In general, I plan to continue with the 4-week cycle, while every two weeks maintaining a regiment of long-distance runs, at least 17 km at this stage.

Looking at the 24k run with a smile, if I reverse the order of the digits, 24 would become 42! The full marathon distance. ☺

CHAPTER 7

My Mantras

Mantra can be defined as a verbal formula repeated in prayer, meditation, or incantation. A kind of a magic spell bearing mystical potentialities.

Some say it is the language of Gods. I would say that a mantra is a word or phrase of power.

I received my personal mantra for transcendental meditation some forty years ago. Since then, I use it for meditation only and I've never spoken it aloud. So, I'm not sharing this one with you.

But for the long runs, I have a few mantras reminding me some of key principles of good running. I will definitely share these with you and will describe them here.

Maybe some will be to your taste as well. ☺ Or, you can create your own mantras.

A mantra should be short, one word is best; it could be a three-to-four word phrase representing an idea.

The mantra for meditation is a word in Sanskrit and has no meaning (for me…), but this is a different story.

Here is the list. Explanations will follow:

1. Be tall and then fall, be tall and then fall
2. Rotate pelvis, rotate pelvis…
3. Iliopsoas, iliopsoas, iliopsoas
4. Brush the road, brush the road
5. Like a cat, like a cat…

Be tall and then fall:
Feel tall. The crown of your head should be up as much as possible. The chin, slightly lower.
Keep your back straight, leaning forward slightly and keep your knees bent. The knees should feel loose.

Lean a bit forward, the gravitation invites you to fall and the legs instinctively move forward to support you, preventing your fall. Let your momentum carry you forward, while shifting your body weight forward into the next step.

Once you achieve that, the true falling, the running will be easy and "self-propelling." The challenge is not to bend – hold the body like one straight piece – as though you've swallowed a long pole.

Rotate pelvis:
Rotating the pelvis increases the stride's length. The pelvis rotation may be supported by arms' backward motion. When your arms swing forward again, it returns without effort like a coil.

Iliopsoas:

The idea is to engage the core muscles. They have a lot of power and energy, much more than the legs.

Iliopsoas is the inner hip muscle whose function is to flex the thigh at the hip joint. It is a large muscle composed of the union of two individual muscles; iliacus and psoas major. It takes its name from the combination of the names of these two muscles. Iliopsoas is the chief flexor of the hip joint.

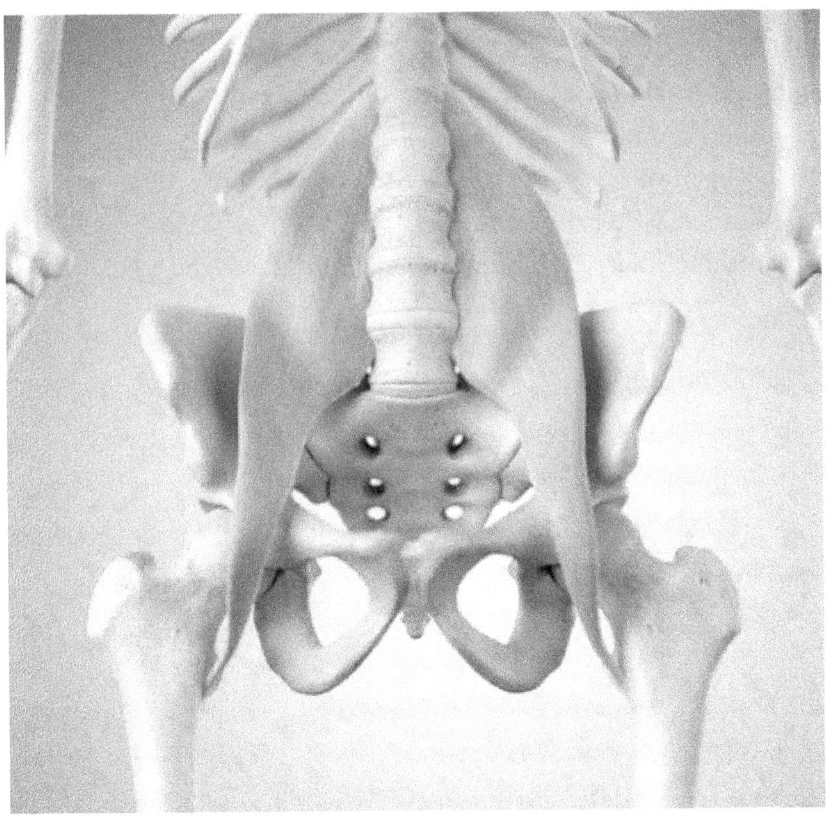

Brush the road:

"Brushing" the ground – I like this visualization very much. For me it really works – the legs truly and easily move back, similar to a sweeping motion.

The key principle in Chi Running is the backward motion of the legs. Paw back like a horse, so your foot is moving back. The higher your foot is, the closer it is to the butt, the faster you can move forward. And the shorter the time a foot is in contact with the ground, the smaller the impact and lower the probability of injury.

Like a cat:

Run lightly, almost as if floating. "Run above the ground" – don't pound the ground.

To feel light, you may use the following visualizations:

- Running lightly, like a cat.
- Imagine you are running on egg shells… stay light!

CHAPTER 8

The Mistress

I have told you only half of the truth.

Indeed, as you already know, I'm addicted to running.
This is a real love! But I must admit that I have a mistress – a "second love." Or maybe it is really the first one?!

In the first chapter I wrote about my addiction to running. I definitely love running and can't live without it. But the problem is that this is not the only addiction I am "suffering" from…

I also love the ocean! And everything related to it: swimming, surfing, diving - and just to be in the ocean, to smell it, to feel it.

Let's begin with the swimming.
Swimming is the least injury-prone of all sports activities. And the one best enabling the unity consciousness, especially when alone with the waves. It is a bit different in a swimming pool, with more swimmers around.

I wrote about the seven states of consciousness in my third book, *Running Back in Time*, so I will not repeat them here. But in one sentence, "unity consciousness" may be interpreted as being one with the ocean.

It's worth mentioning a few of the most important fundamentals about swimming;

- The first one is to be aware of the critical impact of the body position. If we don't move our legs, they will sink and the body will become quite vertical – this will create the maximal resistance. And even if our arms work very hard, swimming will become difficult and slow. In contrast, the more horizontal is the body position, the easier and faster will be the swimming.
- The longer the glides and the smaller the number of strokes per lap, the more efficient the swimming.
- The body should be relaxed, kept as still as possible and be as extended as possible.

My horizontal position:

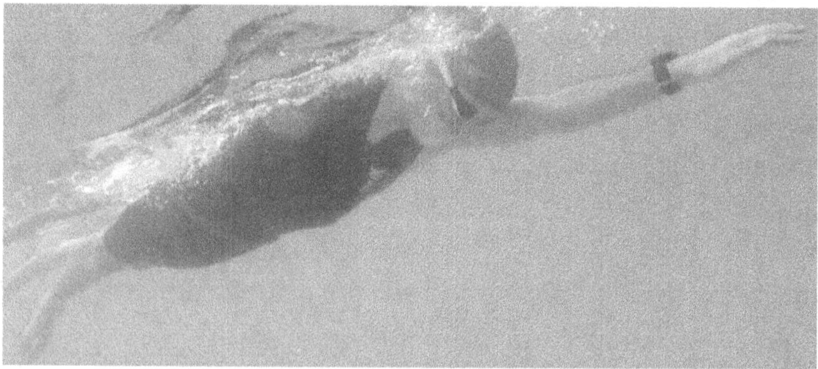

Swimming provides huge benefits to the cardiorespiratory system, and improves upper body strength and flexibility.

In 1936, British zoologist James Gray described an inexplicable phenomenon: Dolphins are capable of swimming at 23mph - 700% faster than their strength should permit. He called it the Dolphin Mystery. Seventy-seven years later, scientists still aren't sure precisely how the dolphins manage to produce that speed, but they believe that a unique ability to avoid drag - they call it Active Streamlining – is the most likely explanation.

This observation implies **the swimming efficiency principle**: "The shape of the vessel matters more than the size of the engine." The word "engine" implies muscular and aerobic power.

For humans – even more than dolphins – avoiding drag is the secret to speed. The answer is in reshaping (and re-thinking) the swimming body.

All objects designed to travel through thin air at high speed; bullets, bullet trains, supersonic planes and cars, share a streamlined shape. And professional cyclists meticulously master "aero" positions. Given that water is more than 800 times denser than air, it's evident that body-shaping (vessel-shaping) merits intense focus in swimming.

How to become a Human Fish?! How to achieve the streamlining?! This would be probably too much for this book. But I highly recommend checking out the Total Immersion (TI) technique, invented by Terry Laughlin.

Diving

Diving is a quite unique activity. I love discovering the wonderful diversified underwater realm of marine species and landscapes.

My motivation to learn to dive came from curiosity and maybe also from my drive for adventure. In October of 2018, at the age of 67 I took a five-day open water scuba diving course in Eilat and earned the PADI (Professional Association of Diving Instructors) diving certification.

Since then, I have dived in the waters of Israel, the Maldives, Costa Rica and Seychelles.

I very much liked the experience of meeting the fish face-to-face, the quiet and tranquility beneath the surface, and discovering the beauty of the hidden underwater world; meeting the underwater creatures - you look at them, they observe you.

Somehow it makes me feel like I'm flying in slow motion.

Surfing waves

When I'm active, but especially when running or surfing, I forget everything, forget myself and forget my age too.

Surfing is the most challenging among all the sport activities that I do. I started surfing SUP (Stand-Up Paddling) in my early sixties. It was a bit uncommon, but still reasonable.

When I was 65 and made my first attempt to surf waves, it was quite unusual. The best way to begin is to catch white water waves. The advantage is that you become familiar with the feeling – how it feels to pop-up, stand and ride a wave, even if it is for five seconds only.

Riding a white-water wave.

The real challenge in surfing is to catch unbroken (or "green") waves.

When I catch an unbroken wave, the feeling I get is a "super high" - much more than in any other sports discipline. Maybe because of the speed, or maybe because of the ratio of waiting, paddling, failing most of the time, and then the 10 to 15 seconds of flying over the water. Whatever the reason is, I really love it!

It took me time to learn to pop-up, stand, balance and to ride a wave. But it was worth the "investment."

All in all, the ocean is the best!

CHAPTER 9

Am I Reaching My Limits?!

June 23rd, 2020

Today I will run a half marathon plus five more kilometers, meaning 26 km, for the first time. My third step toward a full marathon. Eight months to go!

This time I set the alarm clock to 3:45 am. A quick shower, the traditional green tea, some stretching and after an hour, I'm out the door. At 5 am I'm already running.

It is only 21°C (just less than 70°F), so the early wakeup was justified.

I start really slowly, a 9-minute kilometer, thinking about my knee. I reach an average pace of 8 minutes per kilometer at seven kilometers. From the eighth km, I keep improving around 1 sec/km, reaching the average pace of 7:47 by the end of my run.

I am running easily, watching the accuracy of each stride; don't splay, don't toe-off, do not bend at the waist, feel tall, feel light etc.

I pay respect and give appreciation to my knee, running long distances with me, despite the two injuries; I was able to run the whole 26 km without complaints or pain!

Regarding toeing-off, there is a common misunderstanding about the function of toes in running. Their purpose in running is maintaining balance, stabilization and perception of support. Pushing off actively with our toes leads to various disorders and pain in the foot. We should mainly be bending our knees and lifting our ankles – not pushing ourselves off our toes!

After 14 km, I stop for physiological needs and at the 21st km, I stop at the car for a moment. I'm going to leave my backpack with the empty water bag there and grab my belt with two small water bottles, sufficient for the last five kilometers. (All in all, I drank two liters of water, ate three dates and consumed three energy gels. My Garmin claims that I burned 1,712 calories.)

Now, regarding the levels of difficulty and effort. The first 20 km went smoothly and with pleasure. But from the 21st km, it became more and more challenging. A thought crossed my mind – **am I reaching my limits?!**
But I discarded that thought immediately.

So far, I've succeeded in increasing my running distance by two km every four weeks. If I continue with this formula, one day I'll run 100 km. ☺

This reminds me a story about a Gypsy and his horse. In order to save some money, the Gypsy decided to train his horse to fast. Initially, the fasting was one day per week. It went smoothly and the horse looked happy.

Then, the man upped the horse's fasts to twice a week, three times a week, and eventually the horse was fasting every other week (for a full week). The Gypsy would have continued this process, but after not eating for ten days, the horse died.

But this was just a story…

The epic book *Born to Run* by Christopher McDougall is based on a true story. (I'm reminded of this story as one of the heroes is also a "horse" – a person by the name of Caballo Blanco, or White Horse in Spanish.) This is the best book I have ever read about the sport, spirit and endurance of running, and it very much influenced how I view running, and my running experience.

I loved the incredible characters, amazing athletic achievements, and most of all, pure inspiration of the book. *Born to Run* is an epic adventure that begins with one simple question: Why does my foot hurt?

In search of an answer, Christopher McDougall sets off to find a tribe of the world's greatest long-distance runners and learn their secrets. On this journey, he begins to understand that everything he thought he knew about running is wrong.

"Isolated by the most savage terrain in North America, the reclusive Tarahumara Indians of Mexico's deadly Copper Canyons are custodians of a lost art. For centuries they have practiced techniques that allow them to run hundreds of miles without rest and chase down anything from a deer to an Olympic marathoner, while enjoying every mile of it. Their superhuman talent is matched by uncanny health and serenity, leaving the Tarahumara immune to diseases and strife that plague modern existence.

"With the help of Caballo Blanco, (White Horse in Spanish,) a mysterious loner who lives among the tribe, the author is able not only to uncover the secrets of the Tarahumara. He also finds his own inner ultra-athlete,

as he trains for the challenge of a lifetime: a fifty-mile race through the heart of Tarahumara country pitting the tribe against an odd band of Americans, including a star ultramarathoner, a beautiful young surfer, and a barefoot wonder." (David Fleming, ESPN.com)

Born to Run is that rare book that not only engages your mind but inspires your body when you realize that the secret to happiness is right at your feet, and that you - indeed all of us - were born to run.

It is a beautiful story. I would give it six stars, but Amazon allowed me only five. ☺

Caballo Blanco was a real person whose name was Micah True. He was an American ultrarunner from Boulder, Colorado, born in 1953. During the 1980s and 90s, True spent several months per year trail running in Central America.

After reading the book I sought to learn more about the Tarahumara and Caballo Blanco. I was very sad to find out that he disappeared in 2012 and was eventually found dead on one of his running trails in the Gila National Forest in southwestern New Mexico. Caballo Blanco, the superman, the legendary ultramarathon runner, most probably died from a heart attack. He was only 58. I pursued the subject and found a claim that the hearts of ultramarathoners become very damaged by the overload of sustained cardiac output during endurance sports.

So, my conclusion is that the ultra is probably too much.
Maybe it's okay for Tarahumara Indians. Maybe they underwent some sort of an evolution, their bodies and hearts to adjusting running such distances. But for other mortals, I would not recommend it.

Although, I must admit that I know a few ultramarathon runners and they all seem to be in perfect health.

My brother-in-law Shlomo was asthmatic in his youth. Then he began running, forgot about the asthma and ran the Western States 100-Mile Endurance Run twice!
Now, in his eighth decade, he continues being very physically active and enjoys good health.

Regarding marathons, the potential damage to the heart probably depends how many one runs. The impact on our body is cumulative. I believe that the body succeeds to recover from minor up to medium damages. It is hard to set a border line, or know what is too much. My intuition tells me that to run a marathon once, and maybe even twice or three times, with adequate breaks in between is okay. But the more the repeated exploitation of the body, and especially the "mechanical parts" like the knees and the heart, the more that may have an irreversible effect.

Anyhow, I do not plan to run many marathons. First, the first one. ☺ And then, maybe once more. Probably not more than that. But I'll definitely continue with the halves.

The slow pace of the 26 km run has additional advantages; the recovery is ultra-fast! After a few hours I feel really fresh. No pains of any kind. The next morning, I was already in the swimming pool.

CHAPTER 10

The Miracle Of The Lungs

After I ran my 26k, I went to "rest" in Eilat, for a few days' retreat and to fulfill another dream. Eilat is Israel's southernmost city and a popular resort at the northern tip of the Red Sea.

As you already know, I like to dive and from time-to-time, I enjoy a diving trip. But that was scuba diving, with a lot of heavy equipment and dependent on compressed air we take with us for the underwater journey. Of course, it is fine, and I like it very much.

But, when just swimming in the ocean, sometimes we see interesting creatures, and would like to meet them "face-to-face." For this we need free diving.

The other motivation for free diving was to learn more about the physiology of breathing.

Free diving is the natural form of diving – no equipment, just the air in our lungs. The longer we can hold the breath, the deeper and farther we can dive. I took a basic three days course and became a certified free diver. ☺

A major part of the course was devoted to breathing.

Correct breathing is a key element in free diving. Of course, we all breathe all the time. However, many times our breaths are shallow and we don't exchange most of the air in our lungs, keeping in a lot of "used" air with CO2.

Our bodies need oxygen to burn glucose or fat, in order to create energy for sport activities, but also for any action performed by the organs of our body. When we do not get enough oxygen, we may feel tired and less energetic.

The average lung's capacity is six liters of air. We can't exhale all six liters, as the body always keeps at least one liter "just in case", and to prevent the lungs from collapsing. So, the first thing we learned was to breathe.

First, exhaling, a long and slow exhale, but not forcing all of our air out. With a few cycles, most of the air will be exchanged. Before inhaling, release the abdomen to allow more space for the diaphragm muscle.

The diaphragm is a thin skeletal muscle that sits at the base of the chest and separates the abdomen from the chest.
It contracts and flattens when we inhale. This creates a vacuum effect that pulls air into the lungs. When we exhale, the diaphragm relaxes and the air is pushed out of lungs.

Then we begin to inhale, first filling the lower part of the lungs by contracting the diaphragm, and then the upper portion. We hold for a moment and repeat the exhale-inhale cycle several times.

There are two purposes of these cycles: getting more fresh air in the lungs and slowing the heart rate by this relaxation process.

During diving, we want the heart rate as slow as possible, so the body will use less oxygen and we'll be able to dive longer.

I really liked these exercises. For me it is also a perfect preparation for meditation! Not surprisingly, I broke the record of the course by holding the breath for four minutes!

BTW, the average age of the other participants in the course was 25. ☺

I really loved this experience.

I lost the perception of time and also all my senses seemed suspended.
I was floating, with my face in the water.

If we push ourselves to the limits, there is a risk of fainting. Therefore,
from time to time we make a sign to show that we are okay. In order

not to waste the precious oxygen, the agreed sign is very minor, just raising a finger.

So, from time to time, Ariel, the instructor, would ask, "Zeev, are you okay?" But, most of the time it was very quiet.

Toward the end I heard the voice of the instructor: "Zeev, you will be very satisfied with the result. If you hold 10 more seconds, you will reach 4 minutes!"
This was definitely motiving. I held my breath for 10 more seconds - although the last seconds were quite difficult. But I didn't move, didn't make any unnecessary movements. I heard the worried voice of Ariel: "Zeev, are you okay?!" I made the sign. And then I reached four minutes of holding my breath, which was the record of the course.

And yes, I was definitely very satisfied. ☺

The other part of the course was diving in the Red Sea. Once we immerse ourselves in water (, particularly the face,) and hold our breath, the mammalian diving reflex (MDR) is activated. This is the body's physiological response to submersion in cold water and includes selective parts of the body being shut down in order to conserve energy for survival. This way, we begin using our oxygen more efficiently and hold our breath longer.

The other "saving" element is bradycardia, slowing down the heart rate.

Yet, one more phenomenon is blood shift. Peripheral vasoconstriction occurs during submersion by resistance vessels limiting blood flow to muscles, skin, and viscera — regions which are "hypoxia-tolerant" — thereby preserving oxygenated blood for the heart, lungs, and brain.

With this "arsenal" of the body's natural adjustments to diving, we can jump into the water, or implement the "duck dive" technique:

1. Lie on the surface, take your last breaths before diving and extend your arms in front of you.
2. Bend at the waist and point your arms to the seabed.
3. Raise your legs so that you are in a 'Superman' position as if flying toward the seabed. This gives you a low surface area and relatively high gravitational pull, so you will now start to sink without much effort.
4. Do a strong single breaststroke towards the seabed.
5. Your fins will now be in the water so you can kick effectively. Keep your arms by your sides.

Another key skill, necessary for diving without suffering from pain in the ears, is to equalize the pressure in the ears. This internal pressure will enable the ear drum to oppose the water pressure.

There are several techniques but, in general, we simply pinch our nose and try to exhale through the nostrils against the pinched nose. We will usually feel inflation in the ears when using this method.

One more interesting thing I learned, is the role of the spleen in free diving. It appears that in diving mammals and heavy exercisers, the spleen serves as an oxygen reservoir. It stores highly viscous "thick blood," rich in red blood cells, during periods of rest, and injects these stored red blood cells into the general circulation when oxygen levels are stressed and increased transport is required.

All in all, I liked very much this new experience. I must admit, that at the beginning it was a bit frightening, but after some training with a rope, I gained more confidence and enjoyed it very much.

Hard to believe how much we can do with the little air we hold in our lungs!

CHAPTER 11

Recalculate The Route?!

July 21ˢᵗ, 2020
This morning I woke up earlier than usual – 3:30 am.
I'm going to run 28 km and the weather is supposed to be very hot.
30°C (or 86°F) already at 8 am.

The beginning of my run was good. The pace of the first 10 kilometers was 7:44 and toward the 15k mark, it was 7:40. I was satisfied and optimistic.

During the run I treated myself with three dates and three energy gels – a picnic. ☺ When I run less than 10 km, I do not eat.

Maybe it's a little bit of a stretch, but this reminds me of an old Russian war film, *Destiny of a Man*, directed by Sergei Bondarchuk, based on a short story by Mikhail Sholokhov. The film shows the fate of Russian soldier Andrei Sokolov (played by Bondarchuk himself) in World War II.

I recall very well a scene before Sokolov's execution, where the Germans ask the soldier what his last request was. He replies without hesitation, "A glass of vodka." The Germans give him a glass of vodka, and after he drinks it in one shot (a large glass…), they offer him something to eat. But Sokolov refuses and says, "I never eat after the first glass."

The Germans are quite surprised and offer him another glass of vodka. He drinks it, again, in one shot. They again offer him something to eat. But again, he replies, "After the second glass I never need to eat…" The Germans are shocked and offer him a third glass. He again drinks it in one shot!

After the third glass, Sokolov agrees to eat something, but takes only a very small piece of a slice of bread. The Germans are extremely impressed. Eventually his life is saved.

So, what is the analogy after this little story?! (Though I do think it's a nice story.) Well, in my 10k runs, I don't need to eat. ☺

Of course, if the 10k is a part of a 20k, it is a different story. Today, for the 28 km, I definitely ate dates and energy gels.

After the first 10k, I entered a pleasant "trance" and enjoyed myself very much. But after I hit 25 km, the effort felt more immense than ever.

I slowed down drastically and barely finished the 28k, with an average pace of 7:57, my slowest run ever. It was my most difficult run so far.

Again, the troubling thought crossed my mind, "Am I reaching my limits?!"

The thoughts ran fast:
I can't just give up!
Shall I recalculate my route?!
I have an idea! Maybe, instead of the marathon I had planned for my 70th birthday, I'll do what I had planned for my 71st birthday?!

As a chess player, I always plan a few steps ahead. So, my plan for my 71st birthday is completing the half ironman triathlon!
It comprises of:

- 1.9 km (1.2 miles) swimming in the sea
- 90 km (56 miles) cycling
- Half marathon

The three parts plus some breaks will take me between eight and nine hours of a continuous effort.

But the advantage for me over a full marathon is the diversification. In swimming, the legs don't work hard.

On the bike they do, but there is no impact on the knees – no pounding on the ground. And my right knee is my key problem.

Then, concluding with a half marathon. Although, it will be after five to six hours in the sea and on a bike, I know that I'm able to run a half marathon. I did it eight times already, so I do have self-confidence. For sure it will be at a much slower pace, but I believe I can make it.

There is a consensus that I'm a bit weird. But if I tell my friends and family, that I intend to compete in the Half Ironman Triathlon for my 70th birthday, I'm afraid they will declare that I'm insane. ☺

For me 70 sounds like 17… Maybe because the impaired hearing of an old man…

So, for now, it's only between me and you. When they will read this book, they will discover "the secret" and I will have to run away and seek shelter. ☺

CHAPTER 12

Thinking

The pace of my long runs is uneven. There are moments I feel an urge to speed up. And there are moments when the body seems saving energy, maybe for later, and I run more slowly.

Thinking costs energy. I can tell; I do feel that thinking sucks energy. *While the brain represents just 2% of our total body weight, during a rest time it accounts for 20% of the body's energy use. That means, during a typical day for a person like me, the brain burns about 400 calories just to think.*

When we are not involved in a sport activity, most of the energy we use is required to power our organs and keep us alive and functioning.

For example, digesting takes 10% up to 15% of the daily energy budget. But no part of our body demands more energy than our brain. Unlike any other part of the body—the brain runs exclusively on the sugar glucose, the fastest and easiest to burn, and strenuous cognitive activities require more glucose than simple.

Thus, the brain competes directly for the glucose required to fuel our muscles. And the brain always wins.

So, the more we think, the more energy we "waste." Therefore, when you run, don't think! Let the brain rest! Enjoy yourself! ☺

Maybe, just maybe, "thinking hard" can help weight loss. ☺

CHAPTER 13

My Guilty Pleasure

Like everybody, I have my guilty pleasure. The first one is okay, a cup of tea. I drink green tea or white tea interchangeably.

The green tea plant contains a range of healthy compounds that, for me, make it the ultimate drink. It is rich in polyphenols which are natural compounds that have health benefits such as reducing inflammation and helping to fight cancer.

Polyphenols are natural antioxidants which can reduce the formation of free radicals in the body, thus protecting cells and molecules from damage. Free radicals are unstable atoms that can damage cells, causing illness and aging.

White tea is made from the Camellia sinensis plant.
Its leaves and buds are picked just before they are fully open, when they're covered in fine white hairs. This is where white tea gets its name.

Green tea and black tea are also made from the Camellia sinensis plant. However, different processing methods give them their unique flavors and aromas. White tea is the least processed of the three teas. Because of this, it retains a high amount of antioxidants.

These antioxidants are thought to be the main reason why studies have linked white tea with many health benefits. For example, it may help reduce the risk of heart disease, combat skin aging and even help with weight loss.

To make it more interesting and healthy, I add a slice of orange, a slice of lemon, a piece of ginger, a stick of cinnamon and three dried buds of cloves.

In the photo below you can see the beautiful, colorful and healthy ingredients:

In the middle is a bulb of white tea.

And here comes the guilty pleasure…
Two crunchy Nature Valley bars.

These two bars together contain 200 calories! Only 3 grams of proteins, but they do contain some minerals: 110mg of phosphorus, 32mg of magnesium and 1mg of iron.

The white tea bulb, after it opens in hot water.

CHAPTER 14

The Energy System In The Body

The energy currency of the body: The basic unit of energy in the body is the ATP (adenosine triphosphate) molecule. Using ATPs is the body's biochemical way to store and transport energy. We might even call ATP the energy currency of the body.

Computers "produce" bitcoins. The body produces ATPs, so maybe we can call them "body-coins."☺ ATP is a very small unit of energy. A muscle cell can have more than a billion ATPs, but a billion is not much in this case and at every moment trillions of ATPs are used to enable all the activities in the body.

If, by a miracle-accident, all the phosphate was removed from the body, we couldn't produce ATPs and couldn't do anything, even not breathe. So, phosphate is crucial for everything we do. Fortunately, it seems that the body reuses the phosphate molecules, so we do not need a large supply in our food.

Phosphate is quite abundant in foods like meat, seafood and dairy. For vegans like me, the best sources of phosphate are sunflower, pumpkin seeds, nuts, whole grains, amaranth, quinoa, beans, lentils and soy.

Glucose and Glycogen:

Glucose is a simple sugar with the molecular formula $C_6H_{12}O_6$. It is produced when carbohydrates are digested and it circulates in the body as blood sugar. Glucose is a primary source of energy for all living organisms and for almost all biologic processes.

Under normal conditions around four grams of glucose circulate in the blood, which is sufficient to produce 16 calories, enough for 5 to 10 minutes, depending on the level of activity.

If there is an excess of glucose in the system, it will be converted into glycogen and then stored in the liver and in the muscles. Once the liver and muscles stores are full, the excess will be converted and stored as fat.

Glycogen is the storage type of glucose that is formed and kept in the muscles, liver and even in the brain. It serves as a reserve of energy or a back-up energy in case other energy sources in the form of glucose become depleted.

Each particle of glycogen contains more than 50,000 molecules of glucose. When it is needed for energy, glycogen is broken down and converted back to glucose.
In the liver, glycogen can make up to 5–6% of the organ's fresh weight, and the liver of an adult like me weighing 60 kg (about 132 lb) can store roughly 100 grams of glycogen.

In skeletal muscles, glycogen is found in low concentration (1–2% of the muscle mass). The mass of the muscles is usually in the range between 30% and 35% of body weight, so in my case (60 kg) it is around 20 kg, or 44 lb. Two percent would be 400 grams of glycogen.

Therefore, someone like me has around 500 grams of glycogen stored in the liver and in the muscles, which is sufficient to produce 2,000 calories. The amount of glycogen stored in the body—particularly within the muscles —mostly depends on physical training, basal metabolic rate, and eating habits. The full range of body glycogen is between 300 and 700 grams.

Distribution and use of glycogen.
Liver glycogen is a store of glucose for use throughout the body, particularly for the brain and the central nervous system, and serves as a buffer to maintain blood-glucose levels between meals.

As opposed to the liver, the glycogen stored in the muscles is available solely for their internal use and is not shared with other cells.

Energy for sport activities.
All muscle cells have a little ATP available within them that they can use instantly – but only enough to last for about 3 seconds! ATP is not stored to a great extent in cells. So once muscle contraction begins, the making of more ATP must begin quickly.

There are three biochemical systems for producing ATP:

1. Using creatine phosphate, which can supply the energy needs of a working muscle at a very high rate, but only for about 8–10 seconds.
2. Using glycogen
   a. Anaerobic, without oxygen
   b. Aerobic, with oxygen
3. Burning fat

In extreme cases (like starvation), the body's protein would be used.

Using glycogen without oxygen, anaerobic respiration.
It takes the heart and lungs some time to increase oxygen supply to the muscles, therefore the initial energy production is anaerobic.

Using glycogen without oxygen takes about 12 chemical reactions, so it supplies energy more slowly than from creatine phosphate. It's still pretty rapid, though, and will produce enough energy to last about 90 seconds.
A byproduct of making ATP without using oxygen is lactic acid. You know when your muscles are building up lactic acid, because it causes tiredness and soreness.

Using glycogen with oxygen, aerobic respiration.
Aerobic respiration is a process of breaking down glucose in the presence of oxygen in order to generate ATP. Within two minutes of commencing exercise, the body starts to supply working muscles with more oxygen. When oxygen is present, the aerobic respiration begins.

Mitochondria are organelles in the cells that generate most of the cells' supply of ATPs. A mitochondrion is thus termed the powerhouse of the cell. The number of mitochondria in a muscle cell can vary widely between hundreds to thousands.

Aerobic training triggers the creation of more mitochondria, and thus the ability of the cell to generate more power (more ATPs). The mitochondria of muscle fibers produce ATP for muscle contractions by an aerobic respiration.

Aerobic respiration takes even more chemical reactions to produce ATP than anaerobic ATP generation and thus is much slower, but it can supply ATP for several hours or longer, as long as the supply of glucose and oxygen lasts, theoretically, for an unlimited time. This is the system used in endurance events like marathon running, long distance cycling etc.

Aerobic respiration is much more efficient than anaerobic respiration. In each cycle of anaerobic respiration only 2 ATPs are produced, while aerobic respiration, using oxygen, produces 32!

The other form of energy storage are triglyceride stores in adipose tissue (i.e., body fat). Despite the fact that each gram of fat can provide eight calories, the process of using fat as the source of energy is much slower and more complex, and the body activates it only to a small extent, as long as it can use glucose.

If you want to train the body to burn fat, you may exercise while fasting (no glucose in the blood stream)!

Summary

- ✓ To sustain the contraction of skeletal muscles during intermittent and continuous exercise of varying intensities and durations, active muscle cells require a constant supply of energy in the form of ATP.
- ✓ For the first few seconds, the ATPs available in the muscles' cells are used.
- ✓ For the next 8-10 seconds, creatine phosphate supplies the energy needs of a working muscle at a very high rate.
- ✓ Anaerobic ATP generation without using oxygen can last up to 90 seconds.
- ✓ Aerobic respiration begins around two minutes from the moment the brain identifies a significant increase in physical activity, and can last as long as the supply of glucose and oxygen continues, theoretically forever.
- ✓ The body always burns a blend of glucose and fat for fuel. However, the ratio of these two fuels changes with the intensity of the activity. During an intense activity, we use a much higher percentage of glucose. On a long, slow run, we may burn a higher percentage of fat and a lower percentage of carbohydrates, although it also depends how well our energy system is trained to burning fat.
- ✓ As the last resort, when no more glucose is available, the body doesn't have a choice and begins using fat as the major source of the "fuel." The transition to this process takes time, and that's the moment when marathon runners "hit the wall."
- ✓ While it is convenient to look at these energy systems in isolation, when we are exercising, energy will be derived from all the systems, but the mix will change depending on the intensity of the exercise relative to our fitness levels.

✓ Only in extreme cases (like starvation), the body's protein would be used to create energy.

✓ Even at rest, each muscle cell contains roughly one billion ATP molecules, which will be sufficient for a few seconds up to two minutes, depending on the level of activity.

✓ It takes up to two minutes to replace this one billion ATPs.

✓ During strenuous exercise, muscle ATP production can increase up to 1000-fold to meet the demands of the rising pace of muscle contractions.

✓ For the body to be prepared for subsequent training and competition, it is essential that the glycogen stores in muscle and liver be replenished as rapidly as possible.

✓ The ability of athletes to train day after day depends to a large extent on adequate restoration of muscle glycogen stores, a process that requires the consumption of sufficient amount of dietary carbohydrates, and time.

*The key source for the technical information in this chapter is:
"Fundamentals of glycogen metabolism for coaches and athletes"
By Bob Murray and Christine Rosenbloom
Published in Nutrition Reviews in April 2018; 76(4): 243–259.
Published online 2018 Feb 10. doi: 10.1093/nutrit/nuy001
PMCID: PMC6019055. PMID: 29444266.

CHAPTER 15

How To Avoid Exhaustion In Intense Sport Activities

During workouts, the primary energy source is glucose. Hence, it is better to have sufficient amounts of glucose in the body, so it can be used both to supply the energy for our muscles and for other more vital functions like those of the brain, heart, kidneys and liver.

This can be done by taking in some simple carbohydrates once you engage in strenuous physical exertions and the reserves of glycogen begin to decrease, thus avoiding a situation where all easily available energy sources have been used up.

Athletes are also advised to do "carbohydrate loading" - consuming large quantities of complex carbs the day before a competition. Carbs are either simple or complex, based upon their chemical structure. Both types serve as a basis for creating four calories per gram, and both are absorbed into the bloodstream as glucose, which is then used to fuel our body.

The main difference between simple and complex carbs:

- **Simple carbs** or simple sugars are fragmented and digested very quickly. During sporting activities, when an immediate supply of energy source is required, an example of a very convenient simple carb is a date.
- **Complex carbs** take much longer to digest. The classic complex carb on the day before an event is pasta.
- Complex carbs are also found in oatmeal, legumes, and rice.

The optimal formula is to begin with simple carbs, so the excess of sugar in the blood will fill the glycogen stores in the muscles and in the liver. In the second stage, closer to the event, usually in the evening before the next morning's event, the best is to have a complex carbs meal, like the classical pasta dinner. The digestion of these complex carbs will last, and provide fresh glucose as it continues digesting during the race.

CHAPTER 16

Fasting

Any technician who comes to our home is always treated as a guest: first offered a coffee or water with no pressure and with patience.

Abraham, the electrician, became almost a family friend and always drank two cups of tea. Abraham believed in fasts; short, medium, long and even ultra-long. He told me about the book *The Miracle of Fasting* by Paul Bragg, which strengthened my resolve to learn about fasting.

The first time I began thinking of fasting was when I read *Siddhartha* by Hermann Hesse. I wrote a note to myself, *"If you can't fast, you are a slave of your stomach,"* but it took me years to achieve this goal. Like any lasting achievement, the process was gradual and evolutionary.

I picked Wednesday as the most convenient day of the week to fast, as fasting on weekends wouldn't be practical. This is also the day I took a break from physical exercises. I began with longer and longer intervals between meals, until eventually I reached 24 hours break. Great feeling!

Abraham believed in fasting very strongly. When he was diagnosed with liver cancer, he refused any conventional treatments and only prolonged his fasts. Initially it looked as though it worked: he survived for two years, fasting and working. The last time he came to fix the electric board, he did not look well, but was optimistic. Sadly, the next time I called him, he did not answer. Later, someone told us that the cancer had defeated him and his fasts.

I continued fasting on Wednesdays for three years. I really became used to it and could work and perform as usual.

I believe there are three ingredients to be able to fast easily and even enjoy it:

- First, to be convinced that you really want to fast.
- Second, coordinating the expectations - of course with yourself. Actually, with your brain and stomach. ☺
- Third, practice, but do it gradually. It took me a few months to prolong the break in eating from 10 hours to 24 hours.

When I began to intensify my sport activities to seven times a week, I stopped fasting. The body needs the fuel; fasting depletes the stores of glycogen in the muscles and it takes time to replenish them.

There is, though, an advantage in physical activity following fasting, or while fasting, as this is the case in which the body begins burning fat. Depriving the body of sugars forces the body to learn, and become used to, burning fat. I plan to try it but haven't done it yet.

Now I fast only once a year, on Yom Kippur Day. Not that I'm religious, but it is a nice opportunity and also a kind of solidarity with my nation. After studying physiology, however, and understanding the risks involved in dehydration, I do drink water. Not supplying water to the body and the cells for a prolonged time can cause damage to the cells, so it isn't worth the risk.

To summarize: I would recommend that everybody "exercise" some fasting. It doesn't have to be 24 hours or longer. Even a twelve-hour break in eating is considered fasting. There are many advantages to mastering this skill of fasting. It is good to cleanse the digestive track from time to time, and it is convenient to be able to take a longer break between meals, when needed, training the body to burn fat and more.

CHAPTER 17

Losing Weight

Losing weight is a tricky mission. We all know that most of diets don't work. There are cases where people do lose weight, but usually it doesn't last long, and they gain back what they lost.

In order to lose weight, we have to "motivate" the body to burn fat, and the first condition is that we have to reach the phase of feeling hunger from time to time. If we are satiated, the body will not "touch" the fat. If there is enough glucose in the blood, the body will not touch fat. The best way to cause the body to burn fat is exercising while fasting. But obviously this is not an easy task.

The first principle, before attempting to lose weight, is to **balance the daily intake of calories with the number of calories burned on that day.**

The simplest method is to weigh ourselves in the morning and adjust the new day's eating plan to what happened the day before. A person usually doesn't gain more than 200-300 grams in one day, so it's quite achievable to give up this surplus on the next day.

Once we learn to maintain a constant weight for a few weeks, then it's the right time to challenge ourselves to get rid of a few unnecessary kilograms (or pounds). The major obstacle is that we have not only to fight our eye-hunger, or a real hunger, but also the way our body works.

As was described in the chapter about our energy system, **as long as there is a sufficient amount of glucose in the blood, or glycogen in the liver and the muscles, the body is very reluctant to burn fat.** That's why it is so difficult to lose weight!

On the flip side, if we supply too many carbohydrates to the body, once the liver's and muscles' stores are full, the surplus is converted and stored as fat and we gain weight.

Easy to get, very tough to get rid of…
While exercising, we burn between four and ten calories per minute, depending on the type of activity, its intensity and the heart rate. On average, in a one-hour workout, we burn between 300 and 500 calories.

How much weight it is worth?! One gram of carbs is turned into four calories. So, the 400 calories we burned in a quite intensive one-hour workout are worth barely 100 grams of sugars!

The conclusion is obvious: if we want to lose weight, exercise is great, but is not sufficient to achieve this goal. We have simply to eat less. The best way to achieve this is to cut out "the empty calories" – sugars, bread, cookies, ice cream, etc.

I do a lot of sport activities, at least one hour daily. Sometimes two hours or more. During these workouts, my body is burning anywhere from 300 calories and up to 1,000. On my long runs, even much more. But I don't lose weight. That's okay with me, as I feel fine with my 60 kg.

What happens after burning the calories during a workout, I do "replenish" my glycogen by eating well. When I used to fast once a week, my weight was 58 kg, despite the fact that I wasn't exercising.

As simple as that. Eating less, weighing less. No miracles.

The ideal situation for burning fat and losing weight is intense exercise without a sufficient supply of glucose, e.g., following fasting.

After we've learned to fast, and are convinced about the advantages of exercising, this is the perfect time to take care of the unnecessary kilograms or pounds.

Fasting and exercising, even once a week, will bring about the best outcome!

There are a few things we can do, in addition to just eating less:

- Burning fat is a much slower process than burning glucose. So, when we need a rapid supply of energy, burning fat would take too long. But there is a small amount of fat used as the source of energy in parallel to glucose. We can trigger the increase of that by a slower, less intensive activity. When the body has more time to supply the energy, it can begin to apply the slow process of burning fat.

- An additional "trick" which can work is to ingest proteins instead of carbohydrates before we exercise, as the body prefers to use fat over using proteins - maybe an evolutionary defense, defending proteins, necessary for other crucial needs of the body - e.g., if we eat cheese instead of bread before a workout, there are better odds that the body will burn some fat.

There is a common belief that proteins are necessary for endurance training. But the truth is that we really do not need much, as proteins do not serve as a source of energy. A consensus assumption is that a basis of 0.8g of proteins for each kilogram of our weight is sufficient for a non-exercising individual.
In my case: 60*0.8g=48g/day.

Building muscles mass is a slow process, and there is a limit on that mass. In an extreme case of gaining 3.65 kg of muscle mass per year, it would be enough to add 10g of proteins per day.

I believe that even that isn't necessary, as the body reuses the amino acids resulting from breaking down proteins. In my case of a vegan diet, which is not rich in proteins, I can still exercise seven days a week, participate in triathlons and long runs, without any major problems.

Summary

- ✓ The first principle, before attempting to lose weight, is to **balance the daily intake of calories with the number of calories we burn on that day.**
- ✓ The simplest method is to **weigh ourselves in the morning** and adjust the new day's eating plan to what happened the day before.

- ✓ As long as there is a sufficient amount of glucose in the blood, or glycogen in the liver, the body is very reluctant to burn fat.
- ✓ If we supply too many carbs, once the liver's and muscles' stores are full, the excess is converted and stored as fat. Easy to get, very tough to get rid of.
- ✓ The ideal situation for burning fat and losing weight is during intense exercise without a sufficient supply of glucose, e.g., following fasting.
- ✓ **Fasting and exercising, even once a week, will bring the best outcome in losing weight!**
- ✓ Minimizing the amount of ingested carbs is good in any diet.

CHAPTER 18

A Romantic Run

August 10, 2020

My first 30k was scheduled for two days from now, on Wednesday, August 12th. But I added a caveat to my planning, that if I'll feel that I'm not ready yet, 28k for the second time would be okay and will not be considered as failing to achieve a goal.

After using the swimming pool today, I suddenly couldn't step on my left foot. In a quick examination, I found the cause of this unexpected pain – the middle toe on my left foot - it wasn't broken, I could move it and it even was not swollen, but it was very painful.

The only reason I could think of was too much "pointing" in my one-kilometer swim. The pain felt like a 6 on the scale from 0 to 10. I could live with it; it will probably pass in a few days. But running 30 km with this pain?! I admit, I became a bit panicked.

I tried massaging my toe with arnica oil, and waited an hour or so. No impact. I tried aloe vera. No change. Every hour or two, I tried another remedy; ginger, arnica again, a hot bath, even a slice of tomato (someone told me that it causes miracles (☺). The pain decreased to four or a five, but still too high to run 30 km.

August 11, 2020

Today, I woke up with pain level of three. I found two important articles on Google. One article recommended ice as the best remedy. So, I began treating my toe with an ice-pack. The second article claimed that running with a bearable level of pain is okay and may even have a positive effect, triggering the body to heal faster.

I decided to give it a try, but prepared myself for three possibilities:
- Running the 30k, as planned
- Compromising on 28 km
- Stopping the run, if the body signals me so, by an increase in pain.

August 12, 2020

I went to sleep last night at 9:30 to get six hours' night sleep, and woke up at 3:30 am. The pain was quite mild, 1-2 on the scale from 0 to 10, but it was there. At 4:40 I was on the track, still not knowing how long my run would be.

I began very slowly and delicately, observing my toe and the pain. The light pain was there, but in the cushioned Altra Paradigm 4.5 shoes which I use for my longest runs, it wasn't disturbing. So, I continued; the pain did not increase.

After leaving the parking area and heading north, I was alone in the darkness, only some dim light from the stars above. *There is* something romantic about running alone in the dark.

All in all, the run went well. After about 10 km I forgot about the toe pain. The endorphins probably masked it. ☺ The second 10 km were even faster and my average pace was 7:45 min/km, twelve seconds better than in my first 28k, three weeks ago.

But after 25 km, my left knee (not the injured one!) didn't want to run anymore. I was afraid to cause damage and didn't want to push. The conclusion was clear – I'm not ready for 30 km yet. But even 28 suddenly became a challenge. I wasn't too tired; my heart and breathing were perfect. But the knee…

I switched to intervals of fast walking and running and barely finished the 28 km in 3 hours and 46 minutes, with an average pace of 8:05 minutes/km, my slowest run ever.

The good news was, that there was no pain in the injured knee, and not in my left forefoot, either. So, for now, 28 km is my "wall." I will have to work much harder, especially in the gym, to strengthen all the knee muscles. I'll give myself four weeks before the next attempt to run 30k. The goal date is now Tuesday, September 8th.

CHAPTER 19

My Chess Career

My new career in running, which began three years ago with my first 10k run, reminded me my chess "career."

When I was 10 years old, I stayed home sick quite frequently. My dear classmate Jan Kotynia came to visit me. It was 1961 and there were not many things we could do at home. Jan brought chess and taught me the rules. We played a game.

The first chess game in my life, and I won! It was a sign.

The boys in my class played soccer. I played with them from time to time, but I was a very lousy soccer player.
My performance in other sport activities was also very poor.

I was very good in math, solving challenging math riddles, in physics, and in Latin. These did not contribute much to my popularity among my peers.

The best moments for me were math exams. Many wanted to sit close to me, because when the teacher was looking the other way, I would help others, letting them to copy my solutions or solving their exam if they had different questions. I could finish in half of the time, so I had plenty of time for others.

Chess was the opportunity for me to excel in something more, not only in math and in physics.

I taught my parents in order to have someone to play with, but most of the time it was me against myself… It was kind of weird, a teenager playing chess with himself.

My uncle Leon was a very good chess player. When he was coming to visit, we played chess. He always won. No mercy on his nephew… But he did bring me my first chess book. He didn't buy it, rather he gave me the book he had learned from.

At that time, there was no Amazon and it wasn't easy to get a specific book. But this book was his, and I admired him for his chess playing, so it was even more valuable. I still have it. It is over 60 years old now!

I went over all the 50 games in the book several times and knew most of them by heart.

I became quite a good chess player in a very short amount of time and began playing in tournaments.

After some nice achievements, I joined the team of a local club: GORNIK WALBRZYCH. In Poland, chess was recognized as a sport discipline and there were chess leagues.

Pretty soon I became a member of the chess team for the league matches and was doing very well. GORNIK was known mainly for its achievements in the soccer league and all the boys admired the soccer team very much.

I received the club's member card and could enter all the soccer games for free. Not that I was interested very much in soccer, but entering with the card, without waiting in the long lines, was a "ceremony" I liked very much. The life of a frustrated teenager…

The climax of my chess career came six years after playing my first game. I won all the games in the early stages of the championship of Walbrzych and advanced to the finals, as the only one in my age group (16).

In the finals I defeated, among many others, Mrs. Litwinska – the women's chess champion in Poland, a country with a population of 38 million. It was a local sensation and was mentioned in the local newspaper.

Eventually I finished 4th, while being the youngest competitor in the finals, which was a sensation too.

The next challenge was the championship of Poland for the young. I came in first in Walbrzych and went to the finals of the region (Silesia) in another city. Chess was quite popular then and received some coverage in the newspapers.

I was mentioned as one of the favorites to advance to the national finals in Warsaw. This put me under extreme psychological stress.

I lost my first game in the semi-finals. The pressure became even stronger, I made a beginner's mistake in the second game and lost again. I lost five games in a row, for the first time in my life, and it was a miracle that I didn't commit suicide.

There were five circles by my name in the tournament table (the five zeros) and it became a joke that Gilkis is going for the Olympics (because of the five-ringed symbol of the Olympics Games). It was a lost case and somehow that caused me accept the situation and calm down. I won all the remaining games, but it was too late.

I was doing well in the league, but still losing a game from time to time.

In chess tournaments a game lasts, on average, four to five intensive hours. You have to be extremely focused during all that time. No mistakes! Many times, I played very well, clearly reaching a better position than my opponent, but in a moment of distraction, (I hadn't heard about meditation yet…) I would make a mistake.

That's it. In chess, even a small mistake is enough for an equal or better opponent to take the advantage and there is no "second chance." After leading in a game for four hours or so, suddenly losing was tough. Really tough. Even draws were tough for me.

I didn't know how to cope with defeat and each time it happened, it had a devastating impact on my mood and feelings. I began to understand that chess was not for me.

Fortunately, at that time I learned to play bridge and pretty soon became very good. Despite the fact that chess was my "first love," eventually and gradually I gave it up and switched to bridge.

One of the key advantages for me was that in a competitive game of bridge, we usually play at least 24 "deals" in a tournament. So even if I lost one, there were plenty of opportunities to catch up.

I was gradually phasing out chess and became a professional bridge player.

But I'm sure that to a large extent, I owe my analytical thinking to chess, and recommend that every parent encourage his child to play chess - even if he is not going to become a chess master.

In 1974, my bridge partner and dear friend Jenda Fertig and I won all the games in the qualifying tournament for youth, and became members of the Israeli National Team for the European Youth Bridge Championships in Copenhagen.

The European Youth Bridge Championships (up until the time I was 27) were held every two years. In 1976, I was again a member of the Israeli National Team for the European Championship, this time in Lund, Sweden, playing with another good friend Rami Zivoni.

That's it. Since then, my Master Degree studies and especially the Master's thesis, my army service, Ph.D. studies, family, and my intensive career, haven't left any free time for these time-consuming hobbies.

The competitive instinct remained very strong in me, but I couldn't imagine that 40 years later I would compete again, this time in triathlons and in a marathon. ☺

I still dream about a comeback, when I'll have some more free time one day. After all, I'm not seventy yet.

In the meantime, I do play both bridge and chess online, quite successfully. These two hobbies had a major impact on my intellectual abilities for the rest of my life and I recommend them for everyone.

Our three sons obviously "suffered" chess and bridge lessons from an early age. I think it contributed to their high intellectual abilities, although in the eighties and nineties, computer games became a much more appealing alternative and to my disappointment, they haven't pursued chess or bridge.

Many years later, I was competing for a promotion to the rank of a colonel in the army. We were seven candidates invited for a full day of tests and various tasks for socio-psychological assessment. There were also seven psychologists watching us; one psychologist dedicated to one candidate, watching and taking notes.

I liked this experience very much.

We were divided into two teams in one of the tasks. Each team received a box of "construction elements" and was given the task to build the highest possible structure, in a limited time. Everyone rushed to begin the building.

But I didn't. I checked how many elements of each type were in the box, calculated what the size of a stable base would be for the structure and presented the plan to the rest of my team.

The other members of my team understood instantaneously. We began working according to my plan and won the competition. (I like competitions.☺)

At the end of the day, everyone received feedback from the psychologist who was watching him. (Unfortunately, there were only men, no women…) I was very pleased with my feedback and kept the written copy for many years. It is probably still somewhere among my paper souvenirs.

The sentence that I loved above all was: "*You are a chess player in life too.*"

Maybe my preparations for running marathon are also a kind of a two-year-long game, where I always plan a few steps ahead, like in chess?!

CHAPTER 20

Trail Running And Communicating With Nature

For me, trail running is a more advanced stage of running, maybe like a Master Degree in running. Running on trails, as opposed to running on streets which is great fun too (and much easier), is a whole other experience where everything is changing; uphill, downhill, fast, slow… The conditions change in a split second. Wherever I run, I'm out in the nature; on the beach, in the forest, etc.

Trail running has a lot of the best qualities that running can offer. Both physical and mental. Focus, otherwise you end up eating dirt… Pay attention to every single stride. Communicate with the trail.

I love going out to run, I love running the trails near my house, and what I get in return just by paying attention to all the nuances of movement. Feeling my body, feeling the different parts of my body – it's this incredible sense of just being unified with the environment I'm running through.

Whatever it tells me to do, I do. If I need to go uphill, I do. If I need to shorten my stride, I do. If I need to really roll to get downhill, so it that's what I do. I get to participate in my environment. I'm united with my environment; I get to be part of it, part of that trail, part of movements through the trees.

I get to be a part of seeing the ocean and bring that to my run. This joy brings me out there, keeps me searching and digging deeper.

Mindful practice. It's all about joy of running, really bringing my spirit out. There is nothing like it. It puts me so in tune with myself, with the environment, really unifies this communication between me and my WORLD.

CHAPTER 21

The Bal Soup

In my third book, *Running Back in Time,* I shared the recipe for my main daily meal - the BAL meal (BAL standing for **Beans And Lentils**). The main ingredients are beans and lentils, but also some roots (parsley, celery and a small cube of ginger, chopped into tiny pieces, to avoid a too strong taste of each), beetroot, half an onion, garlic and curcumin. If no fresh curcumin is available, then I use turmeric powder. At the end, I add some 50 – 70 grams of tofu.

I begin with heating a bit of olive oil in the frying pan, just enough to cover the bottom and then adding the ingredients in layers, one by one. I add some of these spices to each layer: Himalayan salt, black pepper, red paprika, parsley, dill, cumin, basil, oregano and ten threads of saffron.

My main goal was to create a meal which will provide a significant amount of proteins and minerals, based on the assumption that I get enough vitamins from the salad and fruits. Indeed, the meal contains a good chunk of all the precious minerals and some 35g of proteins.

In *Running Back in Time*, all the preparations are presented in detail and the minerals are summarized in a detailed table.

But sometimes, I feel that instead of a "solid" meal, I would like something more liquid. That's how I came to the BAL Soup.

The main ingredients are the same as in the BAL meal, but I begin with cooking a potato and then adding a few chopped pickles at the end, greatly contributing to the taste.

CHAPTER 22

The Second Chance

Tuesday, September 8[th,] 2020

Four weeks ago, I failed my first attempt to run 30 km.

The pain in my left knee clearly showed that if I don't make some major improvements in my training routine, I have no chance running 42 km.

I again studied ways to strengthen my knees, I read a few articles and consulted with experts.

The first conclusion: back to exercising with the elastic training band, like I did during the physiotherapy following the injuries.

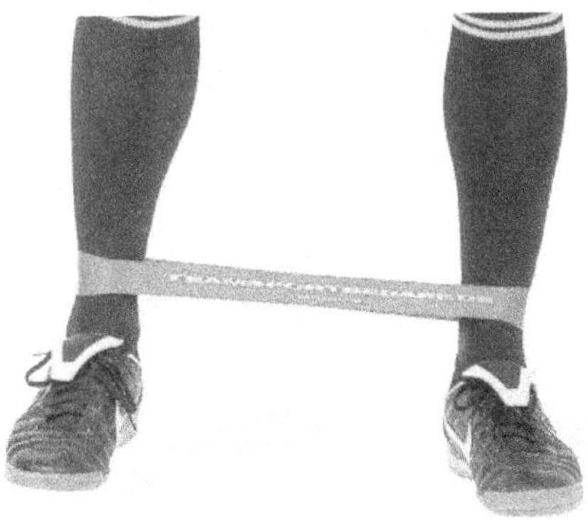

This is one example of working with the resistance band, but a full set comprises of stretching in all four directions.

The second exercise is one-leg standing on a soft-disc balance cushion.

And, of course squats. All on a daily basis!

The last, and maybe the most important, exercise was strengthening the hip abductors and hip adductors.

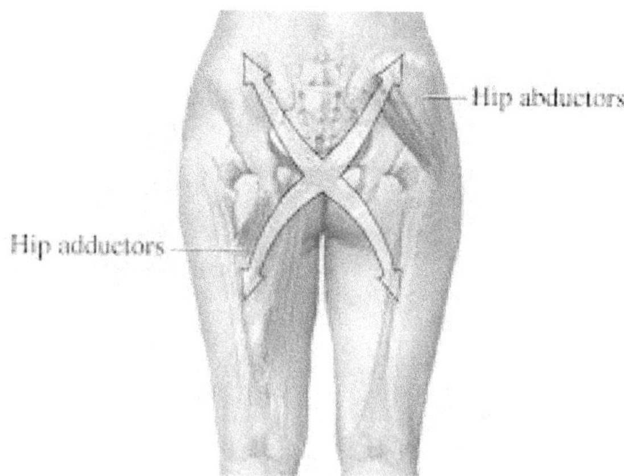

The hip abductors are important and often forgotten muscles that contribute to our ability to stand, walk, and rotate our legs with ease.

The abductor muscle group is located on the lateral side of the thigh and moves the thigh away from the body's midline.
The adductor muscles of the hip, located in the medial compartment of the tight, are a group of muscles used for bringing the thighs together (adduction).

Not only can hip abduction exercises help us get a tight and toned backside, they can also help to **prevent and treat pain in the hips and knees.**

In the gym I added exercising with two machines: adductor and abductor.

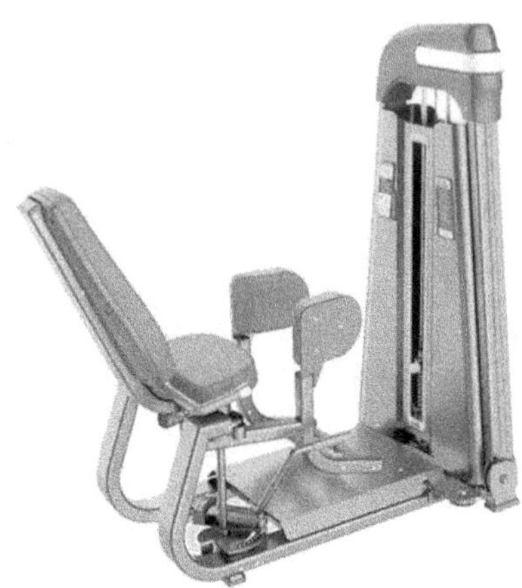

Hip abduction occurs when we move our thighs out from our body by moving our legs apart as far as we can, while keeping our hips straight.

The adduction is the opposite exercise, bringing the thighs together.

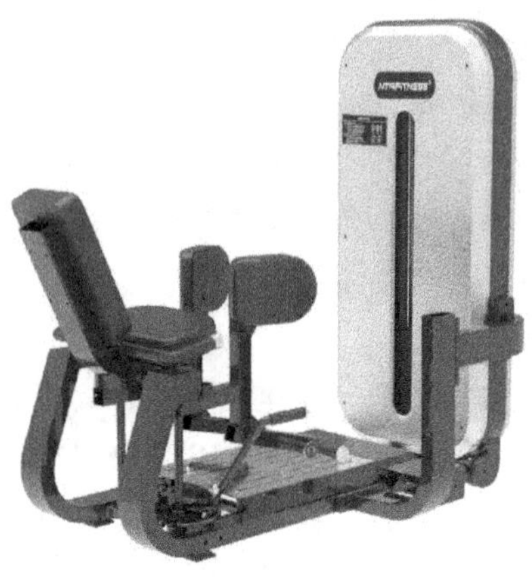

I was feeling good and very soon the runs became smoother.

On the macro level, I had to increase the scope of my training. I used to take breaks before and after runs of 15 km or longer. This created too many "idle days." I decided to limit my rest time to one day, before runs of 20 km or more. I'd swim after the long runs, but not on a rest day.

It was good to see that giving up the break-days not only didn't have any negative effects, but I felt that my overall fitness and performance are improving. All in all, I reached an average of 11 hours of sport activities per week.

Following the four weeks of hard work, I felt well prepared for running the 30 km. I also bought the newest Altra running shoes – the Paradigm 5. I tried them on a few short runs and they felt perfect.

Despite the fact that it is already September, the days are very hot and humid. I woke up at 3:30 am, left home at 4:30 and began my run before 5 am.

The first two hours were really good and pleasant. The pace was quite slow, like in all my recent, long runs in the summer, around 7:50 min/km. I finished 15 km after two hours and felt perfect.

From 7 am and on, the heat and humidity made the second half of the run much more difficult. I began slowing down with a pace of over 8 min/km. I usually drink 1 liter of water for every 10 km. But this time I drank two liters for the 15 km. I had to stop at the car and refill the water.

I concentrated hard on every move and tried to make it as accurate as possible.
Eventually I finished the 30 km in 3 hours and 57 minutes with an average pace of 7:53min/km. I drank 4 liters of water. The feeling was great! I finished 30 km in a reasonable time, without any pains! Satisfaction and some optimism for the future.

The next day I went to swim in the ocean, 1.5 km. I saw people running along the promenade and couldn't believe that 24 hours ago, I was running 30 km there …

I don't plan to increase my distance in the next two months, as September/October is the triathlon season and I would like to participate in at least two triathlons, Olympic distance. As long as there aren't any cancellations because of Covid-19.

CHAPTER 23

The Joy Of Running

The most important thing is to feel the joy of running! First for now, but also for many years to come. And the joy of not having it be cumbersome, or difficult, or anything like that.

When I go out to run it is really for me. When I say "moving meditation," it's certainly not like a quiet-stillness kind of meditation. It's more like a really wonderful active dance. I feel like it's a type of meditation through movement.

There is something so joyful about running that it's one of my favorite things to do. No resistance in me to the "effort" of running.

I know when I go out, I'll enjoy this very fun sport we call running. I really hope that it will happen for you too!

Joy happens in the moment.
Out of all the past (fears).
Out of the future (doubts, fears).
Put yourself into the NOW! Respond to what is happening in this moment, to what happens when I'm really present where I am. Living

in the moment creates, for me, the conditions for the energy to flow, for joy to flow.

The effort disappears: "What happened to the last mile?!"

That's what gets me up and going: I grow, I feel, and I nurture this sense of joy. So, when it is time to run, I feel happy: Now I finally go to run! A kind of treat I give myself!

CHAPTER 24

The Speed Formula

The September triathlons were cancelled because of Covid-19, so I adjusted my running plans. On October 6th, four weeks since my first 30 km run, I plan to run 30 km again, this time in much better weather conditions, and see if I can improve the speed.

According to my long-runs routine, I allow myself to enjoy a lot of carbohydrates the day before, in order to fill my glycogen stores. Then, I go to sleep as early as 9:30 pm to get 6 hours' sleep and wake up at 3:30 am.

The days are still quite hot and I knew I'll end the run at 30°C (86°F) but it will be 3° (or 6.5°F) less than my first 30k.

I woke up at 3:15 before the alarm clock. I took the very early morning pretty easy, allowing my body to wake up for the adventure: A shower, the classic morning tea and all the logistics.

I assume that my leg muscles store some 1,000 calories and some 300 calories will come from digesting the pasta from the evening before.

My estimate is that the run will take around three hours and forty-five minutes. Multiplying by 8.5 calories per minute, my legs will need around 2,000 calories. Therefore, I have to supply the missing 700. An energy gel has 100 calories and a date has 50, so 5 energy gels and 4 dates will be exactly what I need. Nine "treats" for 30 km is a "treat" every 3 km.

So shall it be written, so shall it be done.

Regarding my speed, recently I went back to the basics. The same formula applies to both running and swimming:
Run speed = str. rate multiplied by str. length
Swimming speed = str. rate multiplied by str. length

In running, str. stands for stride and in swimming for stroke. Incidentally the same abbreviation.

The stride/stroke length has quite rigid limits: I reached the stride length of 115 cm (45") and this is probably my maximal stride, given the length of my legs. In swimming, my longest average stroke was 120 cm (47") and this also is most probably my physical limit, given the length of my arms. To reach these limits requires good technique and it seems that I achieved that.

The other parameter is the cadence. For higher cadence we have to use more power.

Key point is, that the cadence at the beginning of a run or a swim, has a major influence on the average cadence of the whole run/swim.

It's very difficult to increase the cadence after the first 20 minutes or so. It's like to trying change the gear in a car from very low to very high.

When I was running mainly 10 km, my cadence was 170spm, which is quite good, and indeed my best times were all below 5:30 minutes per kilometer. However, when I began extending the range toward a half marathon and beyond, the cadence dropped to 155.

Maybe it is a subconscious preserving energy?!

Toward the 30k I began increasing my cadence and the speed improved dramatically. Running 10k was at the pace of 7min/km, still not 5:30 but also not 8:00/km. The last run before the 30k was very short - only 6 km, but the pace was below 6 minutes/km.

These days are "the Corona days" and we are currently in the second lock-down. This time, individual sport activities are allowed and that is great. But we are not supposed to use the car for that. Not sure I understand the logic.

Anyhow, in my early hours, I don't see a lot of police, so I drove to the place where I usually run, but parked a little farther away. At 5 am I began the 30k adventure. It was dark and cold, very pleasant.

The first kilometer is always very slow, to warm up. But from the second kilometer on, I increased the cadence significantly and finished the first 10 km in 74 minutes. Pace of 7:24min/km.

Such a pace would be great for the marathon. I was running effortlessly.

No pain of any kind, easy and enjoying.

After 24 km, I finished the two liters of water I had in my backpack and had to stop to get more water.

I felt so good, that I decided to continue an additional kilometer. It was one of my best runs, pleasant, enjoyable and no pains!

The Garmin showed that I burned 1,918 calories, so my estimation was quite good.

Eventually I succeeded to finish with the average pace of 7:25 in 3 hours and 50 minutes. **But I ran 31 km!**

The recovery was very fast and good. In the afternoon I went shopping - no pain or tension in the muscles!

The next day I went to swim in the ocean. Haven't felt any after-effects of the 31k. But I'll wait with the next run a few days, in the meantime swimming, biking and exercising at home.

CHAPTER 25

A Twist In The Plot

The triathlons were canceled one after another due to the Covid-19 restrictions. The last one, set to take place in Gan Shmuel, was scheduled for October 31st and was moved to November 21st. This gives me more time. I run more and make good progress toward the marathon.

On November 3rd, four weeks since the 31 km, I increased my distance by two more kilometers and ran 33 km! The first 17 km were very good, really pleasant and effortless. Pace 7:09. The next three kilometers were even faster, pace 7min/km. Then I began slowing down a bit.

During the last three km, the legs moved more and more slowly. Eventually I finished the run with an average of 7:17, the best time for my long runs. I felt really good, no pain of any kind and was very satisfied with the outcome.

As usual, I devoted almost 20 minutes to stretching, I ate a sandwich (mainly carbohydrates), took a shower and a one-hour nap. That's it. I felt fully recovered. No tiredness, no pains, no tense muscles.

The twist in the plot.

Few months ago, I signed up for the Tel Aviv Marathon scheduled for February 19th, 2021. It's a big event. Over 40,000 runners participated in the various distances last year; the full marathon, half marathon, 10k and 5k.

I guess the next time the numbers will be lower, but still, it is a big event and the odds that it will not be canceled during "Corona Days" are low.

I began thinking about alternatives. The first one was the Tiberias Marathon in January. The event is much smaller and I had run a half marathon there. But the organizers decided not taking the risk of a last-minute cancelling and postponed the race to November of next year.

Then I discovered the Dead Sea Marathon. It is a quite boutique event and in a very unpopulated area. The more I learned about this race, the more I liked it. Instead of running on the streets of a big city, this was running in the desert! In nature! Along the Southern Dead Sea Shoreline at the lowest place on earth.

That's it, I signed up! Friday, February 5th.
The updated plan now is:
November 21st – the triathlon
December 15th – 35 km
January 12th – 37 km
Then I'll begin tapering – slowing down toward the event, while still maintain the physical fitness.

CHAPTER 26

Running In The Rain

Sunday, November 15th

I planned a really short run this morning, 3.5 km, just to refresh myself. When I woke up at 5 am, I heard the rain. It appears that the weather forecast was correct this time, and indeed it was a heavy rain. But a plan is a plan. As I already said, I don't back off and I do not give up my plans and goals.

I like running in the rain, but on two conditions: it must be a light rain, and it should preferably not be raining at the beginning of the run, when I'm still cold. If the rain starts a few minutes after I begin running, that's the best, as I'm already sweating and the light rain cools me down. But a heavy rain? From the beginning?? No, this doesn't sound like great fun.

But I don't have the time to wait. I promised my youngest son Omri that I'd give him a lift to work at 6:30 am. So, I jumped into the water… this time not in the ocean, just on the street.

It was a really heavy rain and I became totally wet and cold from the first minute. A thought crossed my mind to maybe cut the run after two kilometers, but I rejected it immediately. The thought of not running this morning has not surfaced at all.

I rationalized to myself that if I was swimming, I would be wet too. It was quite a convincing argument.

After a few minutes I became used to the wet feeling and began enjoying my run. I saw weird people dressed in coats and carrying umbrellas. ☺ They had also a weird look when they looked at me…

I ran at a good pace. While my body was burning the fuels to create energy, it also created heat as a byproduct. It felt better and better. Only my shoes became very heavy with all the water accumulated inside them.

That's it. At 6 am I was back home, after running 4 km in a heavy rain. I gave up the shower. Wasn't the rain a good shower?! I just dried myself with a towel, changed into dry clothes and I was ready to take my son.

Regarding the shoes, the best way to dry them is: newspaper, more newspaper and then some more newspaper. First, remove the insoles from your running shoes and then stuff the shoes with crinkled up newspaper.

I usually use two full sheets – one in the toe-box area and one in the heel area.

Let the newspaper soak up the wetness for one hour or so, and then replace the wet newspaper with two more sheets of crinkled up newspaper.

All in all, I liked the experience. And it definitely was a refreshing run. ☺

CHAPTER 27

Passing Through The Wall

It is a well-known phenomenon that marathon runners, at some point of the race, feel like they "hit a wall" – the body rejects the brain's orders and doesn't want to move any farther.

The main reason for this feeling of not being able to continue is mainly the lack of glucose –the stores of glycogen have all emptied and there is no glucose left in the blood stream.

The other reason is the build-up of lactic acid as a result of an insufficient supply of oxygen – because of heavy breathing. Once we used all the glycogen from our muscles and liver, that is the time when the body must switch to burning fat.

In general that's perfect, each gram of fat can provide 8 calories, twice as much as 1 gram of glucose. But it takes a long time to train the body to burn fat, and to switch to this process during the race takes time. In the meantime, we feel that we don't have energy. And we really may be at the bottom of our "fuel tank."

I propose three strategies:

✓ The best one, but the most difficult one, is to train our energy system to burn fat by low-intensity endurance training on an empty stomach and not taking in any simple carbs during training.
✓ More practical is to supply the body readily-available glucose from the beginning of the race! Not waiting until you "hit the wall," but ingesting some carbohydrates with the highest possible rate of conversion to blood glucose (high glycemic index) from the first kilometers. I use energy gels and dates.
✓ As the last resort - wait. Continue slowly, or walk, until hopefully the body will get to your fat.

The arithmetic of the wall and the continuous fueling:
In intense running we burn around 10 calories per minute. In my case (60 kg or 132 lb) it is usually 8.5 calories per minute. I assume that

to run a full marathon will take me about five hours. Three-hundred minutes means 2,550 calories. Of course, people who weigh more will need more calories.

All my energy stores hold not more than 500 grams of glucose, i.e., fuel for up to 2,000 calories. But around 400 calories are in the liver, kept as an energy reserve for the brain and other critical activities of the body. The other 1,600 aren't evenly distributed and legs can't use glycogen stored in the arms.

In a rough estimate, I assume that some 2,000 calories (out of the 2,550) will be required for the legs, while my legs store probably around 1,000. Another ~300 should come from digesting pasta from the evening meal before, still missing 700. Therefore, if I don't supply some new fuel during the race, I'll hit the wall!

To avoid that, the solution is simple: I'll take 6 energy gels (600 calories) and 4 dates (200 calories), i.e., 700 + 100 "spare." This would be 10 "mini-meals" for the 42 kilometers, therefore a "meal" every 4 kilometers, the last one after 39 km. That's it!

The second problem is the build-up of lactic acid.
Here the solution is simple too. The lactic threshold is the heart beat rate (HBR) below which the body removes the lactic acid faster than it accumulates (160 in my case). When our HBR is above the threshold, the lactic acids begin to build up.

Therefore, I'll run, not according to a given pace, but by watching my HBR. Whenever it hits 159-160, I'll slow down. Avoiding the accumulation of lactic acid saves me from muscle pain.

The last thing to keep in mind are our electrolytes (mainly sodium, potassium and chloride). Electrolytes are involved in many essential processes in our body and are necessary for the communication between the brain and muscles. They play a key role in conducting nervous impulses, in particular in brain's orders for contracting muscles, and coordinating the whole movement.

We lose electrolytes when we sweat. The solution here: a pill of electrolytes every hour, altogether four pills during the run. Now, the proof is in the pudding. ☺

We'll see soon, when I run 35 km.

CHAPTER 28

Now Or Never

The summer is over and I've adjusted my monthly routine, running around 140 km per month, in a four weeks cycle:

Week one – easy after the 30+ run, only two runs

Week two – increasing the distance: two weeks since the last long run, 17 up to 21 km and two shorter runs

Week three – medium level of effort, three runs

Week four – easy before the next challenge

The days in November become cooler and very pleasant. I sweat less and I don't need to drink as much as in the summer. So, I'm giving up the backpack with the water bag and switching to a belt with two bottles, a half-liter each.

This is sufficient for 15-17 km and then I'll need to refill on the longer runs.

December 1st, 2020
Today I'm going to run 35 km!
I set my alarm clock for 4:30 am. This is early enough during this time of the year. The mornings are cool enough and the weather forecast says it will be 14°C at 6 am, rising to 20° at noon (57°-68°F).
My estimation is that running the 35 km will take me roughly four-and-a-half hours.

Assuming I start around 6 am, I should finish before 11am, including stopping for physiological needs and refilling water.

I'm on the track at 6 am. It is quite chilly, but I know that after a few minutes I will warm up and it will be okay.
The first 10k go easy, pace 7:17min/km. The second 10k go smoothly, too, and I succeed in keeping the same pace and finish 20k in 2 hours and 26 minutes.

The run is good, I'm focused, no mistakes, no pain. After 25 km, I begin feeling fatigue, slowing down a bit, but continue with the correct posture and accurate strides. I enter a kind of trance, not thinking anymore, everything happens automatically. I'm enjoying myself.

I finish 30 km in 3 hours and 48 minutes, still reasonable. But the last five km are really difficult – is this my limit?! In two months I'll have to run seven kilometers more!

The last kilometers are really slow. The pace varies between 8:30min/km and 9min/km and I finish in 4 hours and 19 minutes, still a bit better than my original estimation.

I feel good, no pain, satisfied.

I'm trying to understand why it was so difficult at the end. I ate okay, eight treats – five energy gels and three dates. I burned 2,124 calories and consumed 650, i.e., 1,474 coming from my glycogen stores and the digestion of the yesterday evening's pasta. Reasonable.

I was focused and ran correctly.

Eventually my diagnosis is that the 5k run I added on Sunday, less than 48 hours before this long run, had a negative impact. Originally, I had planned not to run three days before this long journey. Too much of self-confidence caused me to add the Sunday run. But we can learn from every mistake. The conclusion – next time I'll keep my promise and stay with the original plan and strategy – not running for 96 hours before an over-30k run. We'll see.

After the run, there are five main needs, with varying intensity:

1. Physiological needs, the first priority.
2. Hunger, which usually comes later. But I do eat something light to keep the level of the sugar in the blood steady. The best is a protein-carbohydrates combination, e.g., a Natural Valley vegan protein bar covered with chocolate. Whatever feels appropriate at that moment.
3. The need for a shower. My sweat dries fast and many times, I can postpone the shower.
4. The need to rest. After satisfying the physiological needs, I lie down and quite immediately fall into a deep sleep, which may last between half-an-hour and an hour.

5. When I awake naturally (no alarm clock), I begin feeling the hunger and this is the time for a good meal. It may be the BAL Meal, some soup, potatoes or else. Eating at this stage is a real pleasure.

The recovery was fast and smooth as always. I came home, ate light and took a one-hour nap. That's it. The muscles felt a bit tense, but really not terrible. I had one strong cramp in quad of my right leg during the night. But it passed after 20 seconds or so. The next day I took a magnesium pill, just in case.

December 2nd, 2020

I now begin thinking about the next and last steps, three more long runs in two weeks, four weeks, and six weeks from now:

December 15th – half marathon (21 km)

December 29th – 22 km

January 12th – the run that concludes my two years of training and preparations – 37 km!

Then I will begin slowing down, until Friday, February5th, 2021 – THE D-DAY!

Looking forward!

CHAPTER 29

The Mathematical Diagnosis

I swim slowly. Here's a rough breakdown:
One km takes me 40 minutes. Pace of 4min/100.
With fins, 3min/100
With fins and snorkel, 2min/100

Until recently I hadn't given much thoughts to these differences. They seemed natural to me. My basic assumption was that I swim slowly because I don't make enough effort, especially in the pull phase and because my leg work is lousy.

Sunday, December 6th
Today I focus specifically on swimming faster with a snorkel – swimming using a snorkel is over 30% faster!

I was blown away by the obvious answer!

What is the difference in swimming with a snorkel and without snorkel?! **The head! When I use the snorkel, I do not move my head!**

Therefore, it seems that without the snorkel, my head is not still enough - especially when I take a breath, but most probably also during the catch phase.

I'm breaking my streamlining!! Tomorrow I will test this hypothesis in the pool.

Monday, December 7th

I did the test. My full focus during the 1k test was on not moving my head. Amazing. Instead of the usual 40 minutes, it took only 36 minutes!

An improvement of 10%!

The second part of the answer is in the difference between swimming with fins and without fins – 25%.
Here the answer is obvious too - the legs. But this is not a surprise; I'm well aware that I have to improve my leg work.

Conclusion: go back to the leg drills – trying to propel myself using legs only. Everybody who's tried it knows that it is tough. But it is possible.

Another remark I made to myself: "More power" in the pull phase. Do not just "drop" the arm in the water, but rather push the water, feel it! And then, add a little last push, before concluding the pull.

CHAPTER 30

Half Marathon And Full Moon

December 29th

The second half marathon is in two weeks. Together with the 35k four weeks ago, I ran 144 km in December! That's over 1,000 km since I came back from the ski vacation eight months ago.

Twenty-two km today. I was hypnotized by the full moon following me. I asked him for a selfie, and he agreed. ☺

The feeling was as though he was pulling me! I tried to talk to him, but he hasn't replied. ☺

All in all, it was a challenging run. The temperature at 6 am was 11°C (52°F). The strong winds made it feel even cooler and were a challenge in and of themselves. According to the weather website the speed of the winds was above 50km/h. And they were very strong.

The wind blew strongly over the shore and I got sand everywhere; in my mouth, my hair and my eyes and I could feel it on my legs.

I believe it is important to experience the various conditions; I ran in the rain many times and this time I fought the winds. At times, when the wind's direction was aligned with my direction, it increased my speed and I felt like flying. Eventually the run was over. I made it again. And everything has gone with the wind…

In two weeks I'll run the concluding run and in five weeks the marathon!

CHAPTER 31

Pee & Poop

One may wonder, what about pee and poop during a prolonged activity, like a half-marathon, or marathon.
Usually no issue. How come? Why is that so?!

Even during a quite long and intensive activity, most likely we won't need to poop. But we may need to pee.

During an intense sport activity, the metabolism is busy in burning glucose and creating energy. The basic formula is:

$$C_6H_{12}O_6 + 6O_2 = 6CO_2 + 6H_2O + E(energy).$$

This means we burn glucose using oxygen and the outcome of that reaction is water, carbon dioxide, and of course energy. No solid waste! Therefore, no defecation!

Feces is the output of the digestive system, which is quite decelerated during intensive activity, as the highest priority is providing the energy which enables moving the body forward.

We may feel though, from time to time, some urge to discharge. But not every feeling in the bowel means we must run to the toilet. It may be just a kind of an attempt triggering us to empty the bowel, but not necessary a real immediate need. Wait a moment and in most cases, it will pass.

This "pseudo-urge" appears because of the peristaltic movement, which is like a wave pushing digested food. This continues even if there is not much to push. (It is similar to the mechanism earthworms use to drive their locomotion.) The feeling comes in waves; after a peak, comes a calm down of sorts and you will not feel that urge again until the next peak.

But what about pee?! Burning glucose clearly adds water to the system. True. If we don't sweat, we definitely will need to pee. I can tell you, there is no way you will not sweat in a half-marathon, or a longer race. ☺

CHAPTER 32

From 24 Months To 24 Days

I was hesitating as to when to run the last long run before the marathon. The consensus is three weeks or less. However, my routine so far has been four weeks between one long run and the next one.

The rationale behind my routine was born when I was injured following running too much. I believe the body can recover from almost everything, but it needs time. I was in the Marathon store in and talked to Eliezer, the owner.

Eliezer is a marathon runner and a coach, and I owe him for his recommendation to try the Altra shoes, which changed my running and my life. Eliezer's opinion was very firm – don't let the body "rest" from the long runs for more than three weeks.

I made my decision; a compromise, 24 days, a bit more than three weeks but less than four weeks. That's it, this is the final decision, with a minor adjustment of one day only in a case of a heavy rain.

It was great to run 4 km in the rain, but 37 km would be too much. And I must avoid any potential risk of getting injured. So, sometime between January 11th and January 13^{th,} with my preference being January 12th.

Sunday, January 10th

I planned the concluding run for Tuesday, January 12th. But the weather forecast was again for strong winds, while a day earlier looked ideal. I had had enough wind running the 22k two weeks ago. I made a quick decision and I decided to run one day earlier, on Monday, January 11th. My intuition told me that before such an important and challenging run, it would be good to once again hear the voice of my running guru – Danny Dreyer, the inventor of the chi-running.

I remembered that I wanted to see Video #44 again, out of the 102 video lessons I watched once a week during two years, and I learned a lot.

That particular lesson was about the "C-shape." The first two elements I remember and implement all the time: lifting and feeling the crown of the head, while dropping the chin. This is the upper part of the "C." The third element of the "C" is feeling and almost-lifting the abdomen. This drill engages the core muscles! I will definitely remember and implement during the run tomorrow

Monday, January 11^{th,} 2021

When I began my journey there were 24 months ahead of me. Now, there are 24 days left. So far, I have enjoyed this journey very much.

I hope that you have, too.

I'm in my best physical condition ever, almost ready to run the marathon. But before that, today I'm going to run my last long run. The ultimate achievement would be 37 km.

I don't intend to push. The highest priority is not to get injured. Any distance between 30 km and 37 km will be okay. I'll play it by ear and see how I feel, how my knee feels, etc.

6 am, 17°C (62.5°F), an ideal temperature to begin my run. I'm happy that I decided to advance it by one day. After a few minutes I have warmed up and run easily.

The winds are 20km/h, but the impact is minor. Tomorrow they are supposed to be almost 50km/h, so running today was a good decision. I finish the first 10k easy: 72 minutes, pace 7:12min/km.

But my right ankle doesn't feel good; a steady pain of about 2-3 on a scale from 0 to 10. I stopped and massaged it with a pain soothing gel.

The pain is located at the area of the talus, the front part of the ankle and it actually began some two weeks ago.

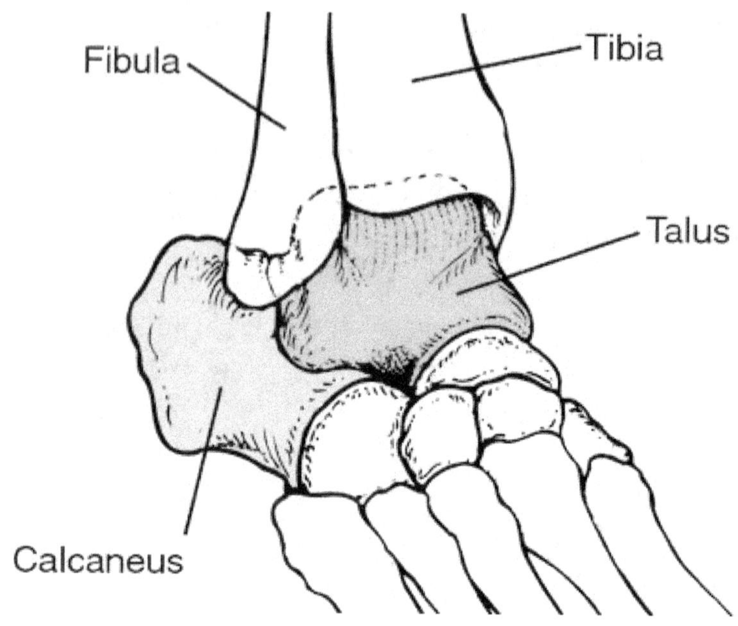

Initially I thought that I was tying the shoelaces too tightly. I tried loosening them but it didn't help. The pain was inside. From run to run, it steadily became worse.

Eventually I called Moti and asked for an emergency help. Moti specializes in trigger-point dry needling - an invasive procedure to release muscle knots. A fine needle is inserted into the skin and muscle. It is aimed at myofascial trigger points which are hyperirritable spots in skeletal muscle and can trigger local pain as a result of a muscle knot.

Initially it felt as though there was an improvement and I barely noticed the pain. But now, during this real test, the pain is back. I continued running with the pain, which wasn't terrible, still a 2-3 on a scale 0 to 10.

I finished the second 10k in 74 minutes and 30 seconds, pace 7:27min/km. Altogether, 2 hours and 26 minutes, average pace of 7:20.

It was 8:30 am and the weather began warming up. I've enjoyed my run, but would have enjoyed more if not for the pain in my ankle. I loosened my shoelaces again but, as expected, it didn't help.

Twenty-two km, a new problem showed up; pain in the left hip and left knee. For a moment I asked myself: which knee was operated on?! But I immediately answered myself – obviously the other knee.

Twenty-four km, the pain in the left hip and left knee became severe, 5-6 on a scale of 0 to 10. I was running and limping. I couldn't continue like that.

25 km - Eureka!
I slowed down and for a moment turned to walking.
Incidentally, or perhaps guided by the subconscious, I turned my left foot more to the inside. The pain decreased immediately. I tried again – the pain decreased dramatically!

I began recalling, that in one of the 102 video lessons about chi-running by Danny Dreyer, the message was "Don't splay your feet." I'm very well aware, that the natural direction of the knee movement is straight ahead, not splaying, not deviating left or right. But I wasn't aware that I don't always do that!

I had felt that my knee was moving perfectly straight. When I consciously straightened the foot, however, it felt like moving the foot back toward the inside.

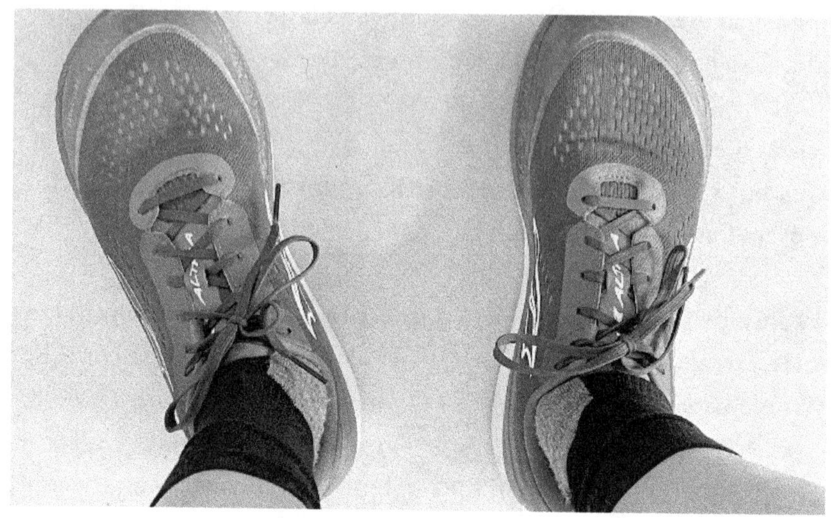

The angle of the deviation was small, maybe 10-15 degrees, but after 25 km, three hours of running with a spm (strides per minute) of 160, it is almost 30,000 strides, or 15,000 strides by each leg. Even the smallest problem multiplied 15,000 times, amplifies the problem significantly.

Suddenly I understood that the pains I suffered on my left side from time to time were caused by the splaying of my left foot.

I always seek the positive values. This outlook has brought me great joy; I understood one of my last "mechanical" problems and figured out the solution as to how to deal with it.

For the rest of the run I focused on my left foot. It wasn't easy and definitely required effort. But the pain diminished dramatically. After 30 km, the run became quite difficult physically. I felt exhausted. Maybe because of the pains and problems?

I continued simply because of inertia, by not stopping. I knew that if I stopped for even a short moment, it might be very difficult to resume running.

My natural persistence enabled me to finish the 37 km. It took 4 hours and 43 minutes, but I felt satisfied.

Tuesday, January 12ᵗʰ.

The recovery was fast, as always. I felt fine already by yesterday afternoon. Only I haven't had an appetite; I really haven't had any desire to eat and I had somewhat of a funny feeling in my stomach.

But today everything is alright and I compensate for my "diet" yesterday. I enter the stage of tapering; a lower gear of activities – less kilometers and lower intensity of exercises.

The tough run yesterday demonstrated more than any other run before, the importance of the training, preparations and gradual progress. We need a lot of experience and time to understand and implement all the nuances of running correctly, running long distances and enjoying it.

Literally at the last minute, I understood a crucial issue in my running – the splayed-foot mistake. One more obstacle is removed from my path toward the marathon.

When I began this long journey 23 months ago, I was worried about two main issues: whether my right knee, which was injured twice, could handle running such long distances without irreversible damage, and my left forefoot, which had been a problem for many years.

The forefoot problem was solved mainly by the Altra shoes with the wide toe box and zero drop. Thanks, once more, to Eliezer who convinced me to try them.

Also, the very professional reflexology treatment by Molly helped a lot. Thanks, Molly! And maybe also all the running; the more I ran, the more minor the problem. Same with the right knee; the more I ran, the less pain I felt!

Many runners have to deal with psychological challenges in order to run four to five hours. But I (or my mind) never had an issue with long-distance runs. I enjoy them very much.

Also, my cardiovascular and cardio-respiratory systems function perfectly. I've never had any breathing problems.

Now, the last issue is the right ankle. I believe I'll find a solution. In the meantime, I intend to follow the consensus recommendation – rest and avoid running.

I plan to return to running after a full week break, and hope this break will solve the problem.

CHAPTER 33

A Surprising Solution

I took a full week's break from running to allow the ankle to heal. On Monday, January 18th, I ran a short 5k.
The pain was there.

My arsenal of miracles was empty. It seemed there was not much left to do; I'll run the marathon with the pain. A friend recommended taking a painkiller in advance, so I'd be able to at least conclude this two-year journey. And after that, que sera sera…

I mentioned before that the reflexology treatment by Molly had helped to ease the pain I had in my left forefoot. I asked Molly whether reflexology could help with the pain in the ankle. She replied that she could try, but highly recommended adding some needles (Chinese acupuncture).

I must admit that I had done a full series of 12 acupuncture treatments in the past for another problem I had at that time. It hadn't had any impact on me, and I became very skeptical about Chinese acupuncture. Molly knew the art of reflexology very well and understood and practiced acupuncture. I felt confident about her recommendation and we agreed to give it a try.

First, she checked very exactly where the painful spot was and pointed out to me that it was clearly the small tendon. When I mentioned that cold was helpful, her diagnosis became clear: an inflammation in the tendon.

It made sense.

I told her about the dry needling applied by Moti, which hadn't helped in the long run. She asked how long the needle had remained there. I replied that it was quite painful, but very short. This led to the answer: for inflammation, the needles must stay in for longer to trigger the body to act.

Immediately following the treatment, my ankle felt much better. But I haven't jumped to conclusions yet.

The next morning, I waited a while before tying my shoes. Will I feel the pain again? Tying the shoes will be the test. I tied first the left shoe. Then the right. No pain!
A miracle?!

During the day there was no pain in the ankle.

The next morning I went for another short run – this time 10k. I began slowly and carefully. Focused on the accuracy of each stride. No pain in the ankle. THANKS again, Molly!

Actually, there were no pains at all. I felt perfect and enjoyed the run very much. I'm ready to run the marathon!

January 21st - two weeks to go!

CHAPTER 34

The Answer!

Following the operation on my right knee, in August 2017, I was told for the first time to stop running. I went for a second opinion, but the recommendation was the same: "You should stop running!"

But I couldn't.

When I had a second major injury a year later, the partial tear of the patellar tendon, I was told again to stop running. Two orthopedists warned me that if I continue, I may cause an irreversible damage to the knee.

I avoided running for a few weeks and then began from square one: 1 km, 2 km, etc. My "theory" and belief were that the body will adjust somehow to my crazy desire to run.

But the fear of permanent damage stayed with me. I mentioned several times along this journey that whenever I felt a pain in that knee, I was terrified and quite panicked.

Now, three weeks before the marathon, I received the answer.

My dear friend Tal sent me an article titled Mesenchymal Stem Cells in Synovial Fluid Increase After Meniscus Injury.

WOW! I understood it very well. After all, I had served as the CEO of Accellta, a company developing stem cells technologies. I strongly believe that stem cells will one day be the key component of modern medicine.

Stem cells are the earliest type of cell in the cell lineage.
They are undifferentiated cells that can differentiate into various types of cells. The stem cells can be seen as the body's raw material from which everything can be created and the body can use them in "repair processes." Future medicine will use stem cells to build or repair various body organs, but it will take time.

This article referred to a spontaneous action of the body, as a reaction to knee injury. **This is my case!** Although the researchers made a disclaimer that this phenomenon isn't very common, I felt very strongly that I was one of these uncommon cases.

This explains how it happened that the more I ran, the less painful it was. Recently the pain fully disappeared! I felt it, but I haven't understood. Now I had the answer! What perfect timing! Thanks, Tal!

For the readers who are interested in more details, below is the abstract and the main conclusions of this article:

Mesenchymal Stem Cells in Synovial Fluid Increase After Meniscus Injury
Yu Matsukura MD, Takeshi Muneta MD, PhD, Kunikazu Tsuji PhD,

Hideyuki Koga MD, PhD, Ichiro Sekiya MD, PhD

Abstract Background

Although relatively uncommon, spontaneous healing from a meniscus injury has been observed even within the avascular area.
This may be the result of the existence of mesenchymal stem cells in synovial fluid.

Questions/purposes

The purpose of this study was to investigate whether mesenchymal stem cells existed in the synovial fluid of the knee after meniscus injury.

Results

Cells with characteristics of mesenchymal stem cells were observed in the synovial fluid of injured knees to a much greater degree than in uninjured knees.

Conclusions

Mesenchymal stem cells were found to exist in synovial fluid from knees after meniscus injury. Mesenchymal stem cells were present in higher numbers in synovial fluid with meniscus injury than in normal knees.

Clinical Relevance

Our current human study and previous animal studies suggest the possibility that mesenchymal stem cells in synovial fluid increase after meniscus injury contributing to spontaneous meniscus healing.

Synovial fluid, also called synovia, is a viscous, non-Newtonian fluid found in the cavities of synovial joints.
A non-Newtonian fluid is a fluid that does not follow Newton's law of

viscosity, i.e., constant viscosity independent of stress.

With its egg white–like consistency, the principal role of synovial fluid is to reduce friction between the articular cartilage of synovial joints during movement.

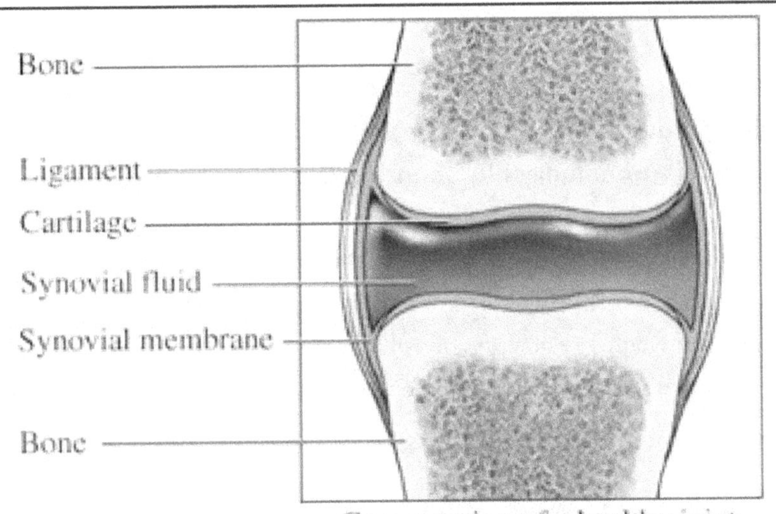

Cross section of a healthy joint

CHAPTER 35

Tapering

Friday, January 15th
Three weeks from today I'll run the marathon!

On Monday, I ran 37 km and I feel perfect. Fully recovered. I'm in my best physical condition ever. The goal now is to maintain the optimal balance between preserving my physical shape on one hand, while not taking any risks of injury on the other hand. This is the time for tapering.

Runners enter the state of tapering two to three weeks before an event. The idea of tapering is to avoid overtraining and any residual fatigue.

The planning should be made counting back from the day of the race and planning the last workouts accordingly; slowing down and significantly decreasing the level of overall effort.

I decided to take a very conservative approach, giving the highest priority to avoiding injuries and not risking the two years of preparations.

Better to undertrain by 10% than to overtrain by 1%, and since it is a very delicate balance, I take significant safety margins. Therefore, my last long run was 24 days before D-Day.

Had I begun the tapering a bit later, like two weeks before the event, I would have come to the event at peak performance. The 24 days may have cost me some decrease in my fitness, but I prefer to arrive at the starting line with very fresh legs and a hunger for running.

The rough rule of thumb is cutting the weekly mileage to half. I run on average a bit more than 30 km per week. I'll cut down it to 20 km next week and to 15 km during the last week before the marathon.

In addition to cutting down the distance, I'll also decrease the intensity of the workouts, the tempo runs and the intervals. It is recommended, though, to do some jogging during the last few days before the event, to keep some of the muscles' tension so maybe I'll do that.

In the last three days before the race, I'll avoid running altogether. The last days' rest provides a kind of super-compensation and will help to capitalize on the long preparations. But how much?! I believe three days should be the optimum.

That's it, this is the plan. Not much time left to conclude this journey of two years.

CHAPTER 36

Mastery

Mastery is a Process Where You're Always Working on Improving.

Anyone is capable of achieving Mastery. Here are the steps to follow: The central rule is to focus tirelessly on improvement.

We have to age with the determination to get better each day. Focus on this every time you swim or run (or do anything meaningful to you). Find an aspect or mini-skill that's just beyond reach… Something to which you must devote every brain cell and fiber in order to avoid falling short of your reach.

If you do that again the next day, you'll be a better runner or swimmer. If you embrace this approach for long enough, you'll also be a better person.

Although I made a major progress in many disciplines, I wouldn't say I'm a master in anyone of them. But I greatly enjoy the small steps of improvement in my running, swimming, dancing, and even in nutrition.

I believe that the true happiness is not in the achievements, but rather in the processes leading to them, in the daily improvements.

This fine definition of mastery leads to a better understanding of happiness.

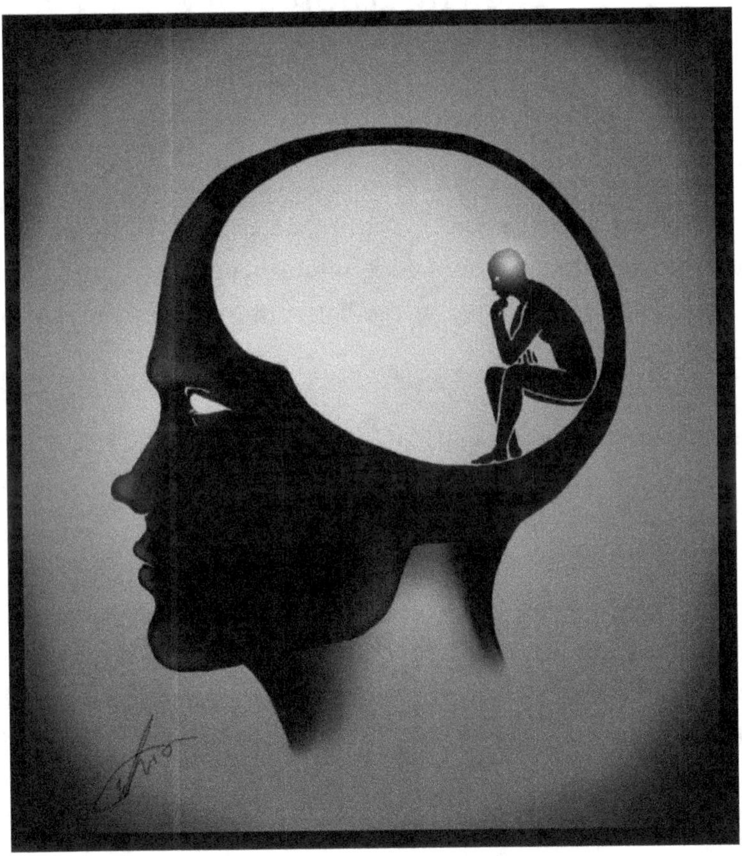

BTW, I wrote about happiness in my first book, *Unlock Bliss, A Memoir of Getting Happier.*

CHAPTER 37

The Marathon Story

The word "marathon" comes from the legend of Pheidippides, the Greek soldier and messenger. Legend states that Pheidippides was sent from the battlefield of Marathon to Athens to announce that the Persians had been defeated in the Battle of Marathon (in which he had just fought).

The battle took place in August or September, 490 BC. It is said that he ran the entire distance without stopping and burst into the assembly exclaiming, "We have won!" before collapsing and dying.

There is debate about the historical accuracy of this legend. In 1879, Robert Browning wrote the poem "Pheidippides." Browning's poem became part of late 19th century popular culture and was accepted as a historic legend.

Although it is a legend without historical evidence, in 1890 it became the inspiration for Olympic long runs. The estimation of the distance of the original route was approximately 40 kilometers (25 miles), and this was the distance originally used for the marathon race when the Olympics were revived in 1896.

In the London Olympic Games in 1908, the starting line of the race was moved to the Windsor Castle to enable the grandchildren of Queen Alexandra to watch the beginning of the race.

The end of the race had to be at the Olympic Stadium, and thus the distance was prolonged by some two kilometers and became 42 km and 195 meters (26 miles, 385 yards). Since then, this distance was adopted as a standard.

Now my mission is to follow this nice tradition, although I plan to execute only the running part and giving up the dramatic ending.

CHAPTER 38

D-Day!

The Dead Sea Marathon was cancelled. I received the message a few weeks ago. Covid-19 is still here and there will be no race.

But I can't give up! I have been preparing and training for two years, and I'm ready - physically and mentally -to run my first full marathon. My mind, my body, my legs, every muscle in my body is tuned to and "programmed" to run the marathon.

I'm going to run the marathon alone! Am I not a lonely wolf?! Like Pheidippides, the Greek soldier and messenger who according to the legend, ran alone from the battlefield of Marathon to Athens 2,500 years ago.

After all, by running marathons we all follow this tradition. Maybe running alone is the right way to run a marathon?!

Friday, January 29th **– the three dimensions.**
There are three key dimensions for being ready to run a marathon:

1. Reaching the right physical condition.
2. To have no pains or injuries.
3. The weather.

I think I'm in pretty good physical condition. I reached my best physical condition ever, although it doesn't mean it is good enough to run a marathon. Anyhow, relatively to my capabilities and my own expectations, I would say my physical condition is at a level of 9 out of 10.

Regarding injuries; following the solution to my ankle pain, I can say I'm injury-free and have no pain! Maybe I'm a 9 because the knees aren't a 10, but I may never reach the 10. Therefore 9 is definitely good enough and it is the best injury-free status since I've begun the preparations two years ago!

I have heard about many runners who got injured in the last phase of the preparations to run a marathon, sometimes due to over-training and sometimes just because of bad luck.

I can't predict what could happen anyhow, so I'm very satisfied with the 9.

Summarizing; according to my physical condition and the status of my injuries, running the marathon now may be the best timing. I'm at my peak and may begin losing the momentum if I don't run now!

The third main parameter is the weather.
The weather is beyond my control at a formal event. We run whatever the weather. That's why I trained running in rain and with strong winds.

But the weather definitely influences both the level of the difficulty and the quality of the experience. Since I'm going to run alone, I can pick the optimal day! But this time of year, there are no optimal days. The main tradeoff is between rain and winds.

In any case I'll run during the coming week. I'm afraid that after reaching the peak of my physical condition, with every passing day, I may lose the momentum.

The weather forecast changes frequently and I'm checking it obsessively at least three times a day. Right now, it looks like the winds will be from 35km/h up to 65km/h during all of the coming week! I decide not to run if the wind is above 50km/h.

On Friday, February 5th, the original date, the winds are supposed to weaken – up to 15km/h, but the probability for rain is over 30%. To make it even more complex, not all weather-websites provide the same forecast.

The tentative decision:
Running on Monday, February 1st with winds up to 45km/h or running on Friday, February 5th with no winds, but with a high probability of rain.

The final decision will be made on Sunday, January 31st.

Sunday, January 31st – the decision.

The forecast for Friday is still over 30% probability of rain. The winds are supposed to become stronger every day. The predictions for tomorrow are 30km/h at 6 am and up to 45km/h toward noon. Still, this is probably the best day this week.

My decision: **I'm going to run the marathon tomorrow!**
So shall it be written, so shall it be done!
Monday, February 1st
The day has come!
I woke up at 3:30 am. All the usual preparations and at 5 am, I'm on my track.

I'm screening in my memory the two years of training and preparations, since I made the decision to run a marathon. It was a long journey and I enjoyed every moment.

I hope that you, my reading companion, also enjoyed.

The first 10 km are easy, smooth and pleasant. It took me 76 minutes, pace 7:36, reasonable. The wind is not very strong yet. I'm enjoying the race and the great feeling that I arrived to this milestone well prepared.

After 17 km, the ankle wakes up. Pain level 2, definitely bearable.

I finish 20 km in two hours and thirty minutes, pace 7:30min/km. I hope to keep this pace up. It will allow me to finish in around five hours and twenty minutes, good enough.

I finish 24 km in three hours. The pace is still 7:30 and I'm satisfied. At 25 km, I leave the backpack with the empty water bag and instead take the belt with two small bottles.

After 28 km, I suddenly feel my heart. This has never happened before. I'm worried and slow down. Pace 8:12.

After two kilometers the feeling in my heart goes away, but these were very slow kilometers and I finish 30 km in three hours and fifty-three minutes, pace 7:46.

The wind becomes stronger and I can't increase my cadence.

Despite the fact that I don't feel any hunger, I keep "fueling" myself, as planned, even a bit more frequently - every three kilometers - in order to avoid depleting my glycogen stores and "hitting the wall."

My strategy and well-developed plan, based on the experience I gained during the two years of training and preparations, works perfectly.

I finished 37 km. This is the longest distance I've run so far. It took me 4:47. It is four minutes more than the 37 km three weeks ago. Only five km to go. I feel good.

All in all, I ate four dates and eight energy gels. This intake of sugars is sufficient to produce 1,000 calories. I assume that I burnt at least 2,400 calories, so I may be hitting the bottom of my fuel tank.

The last "treat" was after 36 km and I can't look at dates or energy gels anymore. I feel as if I tried another one, I'll throw up.

That's it. I have to finish running on the residuals of the fuel in my glycogen stores and in the blood stream. Probably not much left and that's why I feel tired and have very little energy to pursue.

I've been running for five hours. WOW! I ran 38.5 km so far. The average pace is now 7:47. Not much energy left, but my motivation and seeing the end give me more strength and I succeed in continuing the last 3.5 km running! Not walking!

The pace is very slow, over 9 minutes per kilometer but I have finished my first marathon!

I'm flying! I did it. I ran my first marathon! Five hours and thirty-two minutes.

It was challenging but I'm happy and very satisfied!

EPILOGUE

March 1st 2021
I'm 70 years old today.

I concluded two years of training and determination by running a full marathon.

I enjoyed the journey very much and I'm very satisfied.
Is it okay to say that I'm proud of myself?

I feel young and enjoy using my body; walking, running, cycling, swimming, surfing and dancing.

Along the way I learned a lot about running, physiology, how to avoid injuries, how to pass "the wall" and more. But the most important lessons were about myself; my body and my physical and mental abilities.

It was definitely worth the effort.

When I began the journey, two years ago, there were two potential endings:

- I'll run the marathon
- I won't run the marathon

Regarding the first possibility, the scenario could have been that I'd run the marathon, but fail to finish, or fail to finish before the six hours cut-off.

But I had definitely not envisioned the third situation: running the marathon alone!

Now I'm thinking that maybe running alone is the right way to run a marathon… After all, Pheidippides ran from the battlefield of Marathon to Athens alone.

Our well-being is built on four pillars: physical activity, proper nutrition, social life (friends, family, and community), and mental or spiritual attitude.

For me, the first one (physical activity) was the farthest from me until I retired. It took five years and now it is the strongest one.

I have achieved all the goals I set for myself for the last two years and am seeking the next goals to challenge myself.

It seems that a half-ironman will be an appropriate challenge and a great present for my 71st birthday. ☺

I'll take some notes, and if this new journey turns out to be interesting enough, maybe it will serve as a basis for another book.

Wish me luck!

About the Author

Zeev Gilkis, PhD, was the founder of AMIT, an institute for bio-medical development at Technion – Israel Institute of Technology.

For more than eight years, he was the CEO of the institute and led the establishment of five start-ups in various fields of medicine, serving as the chairman of the Board of Directors of all five.

For over 11 years Gilkis held senior management positions at Comverse Technology which was at the time an S&P 500 company.

He earned his PhD with a thesis on Artificial Intelligence, and in addition holds graduate degrees in mathematics, statistics and computer sciences and a Master of Science in mathematics.

Gilkis served in the mythological 8200 SIGINT unit of Israeli Intelligence for 17 years, and was awarded the highest "Award for Israeli National Security" by the President of Israel. He also served as the first Israeli military attaché to Poland and Hungary.

In addition to his diversified career, Gilkis has devoted most of his free time to neuroscience, health and nutrition.

He is the author of the books: Unlock Bliss: A Memoir of Getting Happier; The Secret of Life: A Memoir of Getting Younger, and Running Back in Time.

He is a vegan, and practices both yoga and meditation.